SHAPING REALITY

LOGOSYNTHESIS®
AND THE COURAGE
TO CREATE

DR. WILLEM LAMMERS

AND RAYA WILLIAMS

THE ORIGIN OF
LOGOSYNTHESIS®

Bristol House, Bahnhofstrasse 38, 7310 Bad Ragaz, Switzerland.

www.logosynthesis.net 1st edition, 2024, version 02.01.2024

READ THE DISCLAIMER ON PAGE 282 FIRST!

ISBN: 9798865038986

Cover design and typesetting: Ian Dennis

This book is available in print from most online retailers.

ADVANCE PRAISE FOR "SHAPING REALITY"

The power of words has echoed throughout millennia in sacred writings. As it is written, "In the beginning was the Word, and the Word was with God, and the Word was God ... And God[1] said, 'Let there be light'[2]... And the Word was made flesh.[3]" "Shaping Reality" takes you on an incredible and inspiring journey into the transformative potential of words, enabling positive change even amidst the challenges of negativity. Willem Lammers' Logosynthesis offers simple methods using phrases to reclaim your own energy, remove external influences, and free yourself from reactive patterns. Now, the Move On program presents additional and potent techniques, once again employing words, to help you address hindrances, reconnect with your Free Self (I AM and I CHOOSE), release illusions from the past, future, and Self, and ultimately move forward.

— Fred P. Gallo, PhD, author, founder,
Energy Psychology and Advanced
Energy Psychology

In this new book by Willem Lammers and Raya Williams, you'll discover how to access your mission and connect with Essence and the Matrix. Part I covers using familiar protocols, from the Basic Procedure to Debugging, to clear your mission statement and free your Self. The second part explores the container principle, focusing on learning and growing within safe boundaries. You'll uncover challenges when entering and leaving containers, identifying, and dissolving limiting energy patterns through guided exercises. Leaving a container leads you to embrace the Void, shifting from anxiety to actively shaping your reality. The third

*part introduces a series of unique protocols in the Move On
program. It provides a clear description of how to start, go
through, and tune out, using new statements that deepen
your experience. The protocol enhances your perspective on
Essence, the Matrix, and shaping your reality. I'm amazed
at the simplicity and profound effect of these exercises—
words really do have the power to move energy.*

— Dr. med. Suzanne von Blumenthal,
Trainer in Logosynthesis®, Institut für
Logosynthese, Switzerland

*This book lays out a program for each of us to move on
from whatever issues are holding us back in relationships,
work, trauma, or the past. It is gentle and elegant, although
the process is not necessarily easy. Issues that may have been
hidden for a long time are not repaired in a few days; it
takes time and commitment to overcome obstacles that have
frozen our energy. The wonderful thing about this book is
that it is easy to read and understand: You don't need to be
a professional therapist, coach, or counselor to benefit from
it. The stories contained follow real people on their journey
and the protocol offers each of us the opportunity to move
on in our own lives. I have worked with Logosynthesis for
some fifteen years and having used the Move On protocol
in my own life, I can say it has had the most profound
results in releasing old patterns which have resurfaced time
and time again.
I cannot recommend this wonderful book highly enough.*

— Mary O'Donoghue, MSc.
Psychotherapist, Supervisor,
and Trainer in Logosynthesis®

I had the privilege of editing and proofreading this book. I had already experienced powerful personal shifts using the Logosynthesis model. This is highly effective and based on sound principles; it is one of my favorite go-to methods. Willem sent me a prophetic message saying, "Be prepared for a deeper process than you would expect, even if you're 'only' editing." If by "deeper process" he meant, "Your entire understanding of life as you know it will be irrevocably altered and expanded, and all limitations will be brought forth into conscious awareness, then stretched and possibly transcended," then he hit the nail on the head. This book is a masterpiece. I can still barely fathom the level of consciousness required to have discovered this information. The protocols are a paradigm shift in healing, using the power of the spoken word. The words and phrases he uses seem to act as guided missiles, seeking out everything that is not whole. And then, the light and joy when ... I AM is fully realized... Big changes await you. Godspeed on your journey.

— Eric B. Robins, MD Urologist,
Chronic Pelvic Pain Specialist Co-author,
Your Hands Can Heal You, and *The Power of Prana*

As a licensed psychotherapist, I was intrigued to read Shaping Reality. The book is worth reading just for the transformative questions and the chapter on containers. The container concept has been helpful to me personally and has made its way into conversations with friends and clients. The exercises were easy to follow and resulted in getting movement and some tears. If you are looking for an easy breezy read—flying at thirty thousand feet, then move on. But if you want an in-depth, well crafted, step by step guide for deep personal transformation, then grab this book. I was wonderfully engaged by the authors' reflective questions, metaphors for self-inquiry and their detailed step by step program called "Move On." Woven throughout the book is a spirituality that creates hope and shifts the reader's focus from people, places, and things to an empowering Essence that exists within each of us.

— Rev. Greg Carpenter M.Div.
LMFT Energy Therapist
Intention Tapping™ Mentor/Practitioner,
Sound Therapist

This is an incredibly exciting and thought-provoking book. It delves into the Essence of human existence, encompassing our physical, mental, and spiritual dimensions. It offers a comprehensive model of human life, exploring how we evolve and transform in this world while remaining connected to our Essence. More than just theory, however, the book provides concrete exercises and step-by-step instructions for engaging with these concepts. To fully benefit from the exercises, some prior knowledge and experience with Logosynthesis, especially in a self-coaching capacity, is recommended. The book is written in a way that makes it relatively easy to read, with numerous practical examples. I am deeply convinced and moved by its profound insights into human nature and the world. It has proven invaluable in my personal and spiritual development, as well as in my professional work with clients.

— Christin Aannerud
Consultant and Trainer in Logosynthesis®

I want to applaud the thought and effort that brought this book to life. It clearly originates from a heightened state of consciousness. The opening story vividly illustrates how we can effortlessly let go of inhibitions and embrace self-healing. Despite its apparent simplicity, this modality holds great power. The book is well-organized, filled with reliable information, and brimming with valuable tips that extend beyond physical healing. By addressing deep-seated trauma and resolving emotional health issues that hold us back, it paves the way for the spirit to fully flourish and realize its potential. I wholeheartedly recommend this book!

— Dr. Iwowarri Berian James
Consultant Energy Therapist

Congratulations on your new book! It is extremely inspiring, rich, and precious. It's also encouraging for everybody who is in a change process, longing for tools to move on without fear, towards more self-congruence, avoiding the trap to become victimized. Especially the statement I CHOOSE helps me in everyday life to avoid the trap of feeling victimized: a real energy booster!

— Beate Kircher
Cranio-Sacral Practitioner

TABLE OF CONTENTS

1   DENISE

Denise is a 44-year-old coach who participated in a Master Class in Logosynthesis. When we first started working together, she felt as if she were walking through a sea of thick syrup. Nothing in her life was succeeding; she gave everything she had to offer but didn't feel like she was getting anything back in return. She felt alone, exhausted, hungry for love, and tired of hoping. She was trapped in a repetitive cycle of days that contained nothing but work. After she had shared her story and was ready to address the issue with me, I asked her to say, "I AM," the first statement of the Reconnection sequence in our Move On program.

I told her to let the statement "I AM" sink in and to carefully observe her reactions, then tell me what happened, and then repeat it. She did so. Each time she told me her response, I asked her to repeat the statement "I AM" again, letting it process in her body, her mind, and her energy field. Here are Denise's reactions during a period of about 40 minutes:

- *There is a force, violence*

- *A child wanting to be*

- *It takes me so much courage*

- *Why is it so hard just to be?*

- *I don't know if I have the right*

- *I know nothing about how this works, this "I AM"*

- *I will never learn it*

- *It's hard to breathe*

- *I don't know if I want*
- *I'm so ashamed for just being*
- (Tears)
- *I don't want to be a burden*
- *I am in a place where I don't belong*
- *Oh God!*
- *It doesn't seem to make sense*
- (Sighs)
- *It is difficult for me*
- *Nobody would see I am*
- *I am very afraid, but I am!*
- (In a defiant tone) *If I manage or not!*
- *I am!*

Willem: *Welcome!*

What happened during this sequence? Denise told me the story about how hopeless and lonely she felt after years of struggling in her love relationship, in her profession, in her health, and in her finances. She was in a state of despondency and despair. During 20 iterations of a short statement, she went through a wide range of reactions in response to that statement, from despondency to utter joy. In the beginning she doubted her right to even exist, equating this right with what others thought she should do, think, or be. However, by persisting, she began to access a new level of energy and power that enabled her to get back on track, to see the way forward, to take responsibility for her life, and to find the energy to act.

Denise's life started to change from this session on. As she worked her way through the program in this book, a long series of small coincidences began to happen to her and around her, until she finally realized that she was the one shaping her reality.

The Move On program starts with a simple statement: "I AM." These two words can open your life up to a meaningful new way of being. How? We'll tell you.

PREFACE

Is this but a dream?
Shadows shift in silent thought,
Reality takes form.

This book has been an exercise in courage from the beginning to the end. During the pandemic I published three other books, and in retrospect, I feel that authoring them was a breeze compared with the challenges I've gone through with Raya while working on this book. Since this is about the courage to create, I'll describe my journey in those terms.

The courage to learn

After *Alone to Alive*, I reduced my seminar activities and handed over some roles I had played in the Logosynthesis community. What followed was a fog, emptiness. I tumbled into the Void and needed to find the courage to learn something new. After discovering the *Bridge to Eternity* (described in *Alone to Alive*), I knew that there was more to learn in this field but didn't have a clue where to start searching for it. Raya and I had long discussions, and slowly the Move On protocol crystallized. I realized that this way of working went far beyond the classical applications of Logosynthesis in which an issue is identified, activated, and resolved via a relatively simple procedure.

The courage to practice

From there, we needed the courage to start practicing and exploring these ideas in contact with other human beings.

I invited people from the Logosynthesis community to join us and to practice the protocol in small groups. We were thrilled by the impact of the program on the participants: Those who really engaged in the program went through deep changes. While the final results were encouraging, the protocol often brought old pain up to the surface level of consciousness to be dealt with. We developed the program further with the help of Lily, Cathy, Chloe, and other dedicated colleagues and friends. For a while, we were not even sure if we should publish this material as a book. It was only after I taught a group of experienced Logosynthesis practitioners a Move On Master Class that we made this decision.

The courage to act

After that Master Class, I felt stuck for months, and needed to call upon another type of courage. There were a lot of questions in my mind. Did I want to publish a book with a program that can lead to distress and discomfort before an issue can be resolved? Did I want to take the risk that people could get hurt, or that they might be overwhelmed by what came up for them? Was this an ethical thing to do? I sought advice from friends and colleagues. Some said that I shouldn't take the risk, others told me that everyone is responsible for their own growth and development. Those discussions caused us to thoroughly review all three parts of the book, especially the steps of the Move On protocol. We found ways to soften its effects by structuring the steps, slowing down the process, and describing possible pitfalls with ways to resolve them. If you're reading this book now, it means that we've found the courage to act.

The courage to let go

After this book is published, there is nothing more we can do, and we must let go. A book takes on a life of its own, independent of its authors. From the date of publication, people decide to buy and read the book. If they read it, it's up to them to interpret its content and exercises. Once I've let go, a new manifestation of the Void will appear, clearing a space in which yet another book will be created.

The courage to play

The courage to play is possibly the most important in a project like this. A book is not just written at a desk sitting in front of a screen. Off screen time is just as important: meeting people, walking in nature, or even watching TV and playing computer games. This facet became most clear in my conversations with Raya. If we didn't feel motivated, we accepted that state, and we spent time talking about everything but the book. Playing allowed us to return to the keyboard and the screen when the time was right.

My mission

Through the years, my mission in life has crystallized as serving people in their process of healing and development—in the most gentle and elegant way possible. It has taken me a long time to reach that clarity, a time during which I've played in many fields—in my profession as a psychologist, a psychotherapist, a coach, and a trainer, and privately in landscape photography. Only recently have I realized that it's my mission—and my passion—to reduce complexity for people who are looking to find solace and healing on their life path.

That feels completely true, and now I can understand what Sigmund Freud meant in his letter to his friend Wilhelm Fliess:

> *A man like me cannot live without a hobbyhorse, a consuming passion—in Schiller's words a tyrant. I have found my tyrant, and in his service, I know no limits. My tyrant is psychology.*[4]

If I look back upon the past 73 years, it's amazing how following my calling has brought me into contact with the people and resources that made it possible to spread the word about my work. And now, I'm still exploring, with Rainer Maria Rilke:

> *I live my life in widening circles that reach out across the world. I may not complete this last one but I will give myself to it.*[5]

This book doesn't pretend to deliver answers, but it will create spaces for your passion.

Maienfeld, Switzerland, in the fall of 2023, after the first snow has fallen on the top of the mountains,

Willem.

I have gone from rags to riches in the sorrow of the night
In the violence of a summer's dream, in the chill of a wintery light
And the bitter dance of loneliness fading into space
In the broken veil of innocence on each forgotten face.
I hear the aging footsteps like the motion of the sea.
Sometimes I turn, there's someone there, other times its only me,
I am hanging in the balance of the reality of man—
Like every sparrow falling, like every grain of sand.
— Bob Dylan[6]

When we started writing this book, I approached it from the perspective that this was a book for "other people." It wasn't for me because I had already moved on from a lot of the things that had negatively impacted me in my life. I am a great believer in people working on their stuff, doing their own inner work, and I have been doing that for a good number of years. Then, at the end of 2022, my friend hung himself in a closet late one Thursday. Just like that. One day he was here, and then he was gone.

It takes a split second for your energy to freeze. It can happen so fast that your thinking mind doesn't even register it. In the months that followed, I hurtled round on the rollercoaster of grief: anger, depression, recrimination, tears, and laughter. For a long time, I felt as if I were living behind a pane of glass, disconnected from normal life, even though I tried very hard to get on with it. Sometimes it was hard to write about Moving On while I couldn't see how that would be possible, and I wasn't sure I wanted to anyway...

Moving On had suddenly become important, but I wasn't going to be able to move on if I minimized the situation. I needed to first acknowledge what was really going on deep down inside in my inner world.

This Move On program provides a pathway for a great many situations, not only for grief. This pathway is not always easy. This protocol is not like the sentences of the Logosynthesis Basic Procedure, it isn't exhilarating like Debugging can be, and it isn't serene like the Bridge to Eternity.

Willem and I had regular Zoom calls to discuss progress, ideas, and the testing that our colleagues kindly offered to help us with. We also tried various options ourselves over long and short time periods. There was one Zoom call where we concluded that this protocol wasn't like being on the bus, it was more like being thrown under it and run over a few times! There were times it felt worse before it felt better; but when it did feel better, the healing and the relief were like nothing else. We also had an intense week in Bad Ragaz where even our editing process Moved On! Editing is complicated, there's a lot to juggle and the potential for arguments and conflict looms large—especially when working in a small space. Fortunately, we didn't have any major disagreements and worked in a harmony that we hadn't experienced before, and it surprised even us. We also experienced 36 hours of non-stop rain, some serene walks in the mountains, and the very best food…

This is more than a book and more than just another protocol. It goes deep. It touches on issues that you are not aware of at the time you begin the program, and it can upset your applecart. It can be time consuming and messy. The good news is that it quickly improves if you stick with the process and are willing to seek support if you need it. The benefits far outweigh any temporary discomfort.

Clarity changes a lot of things. Clearing old baggage frees up a lot of energy. Knowing what you want removes distractions and makes decisions easy. Move On does all this. It doesn't matter if your issue is a relationship, a work conflict, pain from the past, or a seemingly unsolvable problem. Move On will move you on.

I have slowly incorporated this protocol into my not quite daily practice; sometimes I use a single phrase, other times a whole sequence resonates. I rarely finish the whole thing.

This was originally supposed to be a book exclusively about creativity; it has turned into so much more than that! I still use it for creative conundrums all the time though: How to finish a painting, how to get unstuck when writing a chapter, how to make dinner when I forget an important ingredient… the results are never what you think!

We debated whether to publish this, questioned whether it was too intense, too extreme, too much… Now that it is a book, I am anticipating hearing many stories from our community and from the wider public about the events and transformations that happen because of this particular application of Logosynthesis.

I hope you enjoy this book, and that you Move On to achieve, to attain and to be everything that you are here for.

Much love,
Raya.

4   SIGNPOSTS

4.1 The parts of this book

This book is divided into three parts. Part I helps you locate your current position and become aware of your purpose. You can't move on if you don't know where you are and where you want to go. Awareness of your purpose will activate your creative potential—automatically. This part of the book contains exercises and questions to help you discover or refine your personal and spiritual path.

Part II of this book introduces you to a helpful concept for growth and development—Wilfred Bion's *container/contained* model. Throughout your life, your environment provides a series of containers or cocoons that serve as holding and learning environments for you. You enter, stay for a while, and eventually leave these containers as you grow and progress through life. Each container protects you and offers a space for growth, until it's time to move on. Leaving a protective cocoon rarely leads to immediate safety. Venturing into the unknown, the Void, can evoke intense emotions—loneliness, shame, guilt, nostalgia, grief, confusion, fear, relief, hope, curiosity, or sheer joy. These emotions may stem from painful past events or reconnect you to earlier joyful experiences. In both cases, you need courage to navigate and overcome as you journey towards your next destination. It will be more distressing to move forward if the past has limited your freedom and curiosity.

Part III presents a new and fascinating Logosynthesis program: *Move On*. We have designed it to help you to become aware of your mission, overcome fear, traverse the Void, perceive a new reality, and then shape it. It works regardless of adversity, uncertainty, or how long you have been hesitating.

The protocol in part III of the book will support you in connecting with your Essence, in activating your Free Self to overcome whatever stands in the way of your healing and development, and to discover new people and resources in the Matrix. It does not matter if you are facing a significant irreversible life change, like the loss of a relative or a job. It does not matter if you are seeking a new strategy for your business or wishing to repair a difficult relationship. Regardless of what you are looking for, the program offers a wealth of practical exercises and guidance to help you unlock your true potential and tap into the wealth of creative energy that resides within you. We recommend reading part III in its entirety before you proceed with its application, including the reports of people who have already done it.

The Move On program is intense. It is different from previous Logosynthesis programs and protocols. It may not offer the immediate relief that comes with applying the Basic Procedure or other techniques, and you may feel worse before you feel better. In the end, it will help you to resolve persistent issues at an extremely deep level. You need patience in this work; you cannot resolve what you have been carrying around for 40 years in 40 minutes. However, 40 hours or 40 days will likely open doors to significant change.

Your transformation may have already begun when you discovered this book or while reading these initial lines. This first content may have already activated issues that are currently beyond your awareness. You might notice this as procrastination, irritation, distraction, anxiety, or wandering thoughts. The mere presence of such reactions, perhaps counterintuitively, can indicate that you've already touched on an issue that you need to address. If you encounter such effects, slow down and explore what is happening. Eventually, you'll recognize which reactions mark the beginning of the process you intend.

In the text, "We" refers to a shared experience of all human beings. The word "we" can also mean that Raya and I developed the idea, paragraph, or chapter together. "I" indicates that Willem is writing from his knowledge and experience.

UNCHARTED
TERRITORY

Here is a test to find out
whether your mission in life is complete.
If you're alive, it isn't.
— Lauren Bacall[7]

5.1 The Land of Don't Know

You're moving, entering uncharted territory. There is a blank spot on your map, an unfamiliar world. You enter realms that leave you blind and speechless, and you lack words, concepts, or images to even put things into context.

You react to these unknown worlds, oscillating between fright, flight, patience, curiosity, and bright enthusiasm. Your body resonates—with excitement, tension, excruciating pain, numbness, or freezing.

You start recognizing patterns: reading the tracks and picking up signals. You try to understand the new world from the reservoir of your previous knowledge, with your experience. But this doesn't work here.

You get help from others in your world, from parents, teachers, managers, supervisors, and trainers. People show you the way in this unknown terrain. They know others and they know languages, techniques, risks, chances, and shortcuts. They help you to translate your new experiences into knowledge.

Your Essence, that everlasting You, has provided you with a mission for this life. Your body and mind are your tools to accomplish this mission, but first you must learn and practice the language, the skills, the codes, and the rules that you need to find your way in the world.

At the beginning of your journey there is only a vague sense of meaning, an unclear assignment signaling faintly from within. If you're like most people, your mission first appears in these vague forms and contours. Over time, and through many iterations of trial and error, you begin to gain focus. One idea is confirmed, and another is rejected. You choose one thing, while avoiding another. You spend your life discovering, learning, experiencing, and stepping back.

5.2 What we have learned

You're more than a body with a mind. You're a being beyond space and time, always expanding. You have arrived on planet Earth in an environment we like to call the Matrix, a temporary laboratory for the evolution of your soul through the ages. Living as a body and a mind in this world is an overwhelming experience, to the point where you can even lose contact with your timeless nature and the reason why you're here to begin with.

With conception and birth, a journey ensues on a long and winding road during which you must reconnect with your eternal nature and become aware of your mission in this place. You then must explore the world around you and connect with the Matrix, in order to fulfill this mission.

In my book *Sparks at Dawn*, I describe how you enter life on Earth and how you can lose contact with your mission while on that path. In the book *Alone to Alive*, Raya and I have shown how you can get caught in a spider web of beliefs that limit your growth and potential and how you can get out of that web.

Both books offer strategies to resolve frozen energy patterns that stand in the way of fully becoming and expressing what you already are: a divine being with a mission on this planet. In the movie The Matrix and its sequels, the Matrix is an all-encompassing system that thrives on the energy of humanity that's populating it. The Matrix consumes people's life energy in exchange for satisfying the needs of their minds and their bodies, making their lives safe and predictable. Real life is not much different. Keanu Reeves, the star of the series, is reported to have said:

The Matrix is not science fiction; it's a documentary.

Through our work with Logosynthesis, we have discovered that you don't need to be a faint-hearted servant of the Matrix and its inhabitants. You are capable of so much more than just surviving and satisfying your basic needs. Once you recognize the deeper meaning and purpose of your life, you will experience a greater sense of fulfillment than any programmed experience can ever provide. You no longer need to sacrifice your energy and freedom in exchange for the safety of your body and the entertainment of your mind.

There is more to life than the specific area of the Matrix you have chosen to reside in. There is an eternal You, unfolding on a journey that's uniquely yours, a hero's journey where you expand the consciousness of your everlasting being. By utilizing the power of words in Logosynthesis, you can uncover deeper meaning in your life and find a sense of peace and purpose that transcends everyday struggles. So don't sell yourself short—embrace your true potential and dare to discover some of the rich nuances that life has to offer.

We will not tell you to follow us in the same way that Morpheus invited Neo to follow him in that iconic scene in the first Matrix movie.[8] However, we will provide you with a set of ideas, instructions, and tools to navigate the Void that will inevitable appear as you start questioning the world that you have come to believe with your eyes. It takes courage to leave the beaten tracks of the Matrix; it takes courage to move on from the places that you have been stuck in.

From its inception in 2005, Logosynthesis has provided a marvelous model to help people overcome painful memories from the past, paralyzing fantasies about the future, and limiting beliefs in the present. *Alone to Alive* opened the door to activating your unique potential by showing various ways of dismantling outdated introjects and beliefs. It also addressed the Void and how to navigate it with the help of the Bridge to Eternity.

This book will guide you in an alternative way of facing the Void and in touring the fascinating vistas that lie beyond it. In that new world, the same Matrix that's been limiting you will begin to serve you on the path of finding and fulfilling your life purpose. As you move on from here, you'll be surprised at what the Matrix has to offer in the service of your mission, once you choose to open your eyes.

This book does not provide a map of the landscapes of your life; in that sense, it's not a classical self-help book. You're the one who will plot and draw the map that you need. In the words of Antonio Machado, the Spanish poet:

> *Traveler, there is no path;*
> *the path is made by walking.*[9]

5.3 Life as you know it

Your life is an continuous act of creation, from the moment you're born on this planet. As you move through life, you influence and shape the world around you. Your birth (by definition) transformed a couple into parents or a child into a sibling; you built connections, formed a career, met a lover, perhaps became a parent and later a grandparent. Along the way you created a network of family members, friends, colleagues, competitors, and maybe even a few enemies.

As you shape the world, the world also begins to shape you. You learn the language spoken in your land, and you move through the required stages of education and socialization, taking on concurrent roles as a child, sibling, pupil, friend, student, partner, parent, caretaker, employee, colleague, boss, or entrepreneur. You learn the codes and rules that govern your social environment and society, and you become familiar and proficient with the workings of the Matrix.

You develop an understanding of these rules, and you pass them down to the next generation, thus ensuring that the cycle of creation and growth continues. As you navigate the world, you add to its stability and to its evolution. Within this interaction, it's your task to access the energy to shape your own destiny and influence the world around you. You also need to create a space for your unique Essence in the world of form.

As you start grasping different aspects of life, you move through a continuous loop of learning, practicing, mastering, and letting go. With each new relationship, role or job, life brings new challenges, opportunities and demands. Growth is neither smooth nor linear, and patterns only become clear in retrospect. You experience transitions, most notably when your environment changes. Each time this happens, there is a sometimes painful letting go of the past, and a slow acceptance of the challenges ahead.

It takes courage to move on. You give up the identity of the person you have been in exchange for roles you have never played before. I can sympathize with any man or woman, young or old, who keeps hanging on in a situation that's uncomfortable or limiting. It can be scarier to leave the familiar misery of a loveless relationship or an unfulfilling job than to face the unknown and the uncertain: the Void.

Every day, whether you like it or not, you create and shape the world of form, the look and feel of your life. You shape it through your response of fear or curiosity, by choosing to repeat familiar patterns on solid ground, or to cross a bridge to the Land of Don't Know. In shaping reality, you move from fear to courage and back—again and again.

This book is designed to encourage and empower you to overcome your fear and to move on; to take the lead in shaping your reality, with the support of this comprehensive program. It describes the nature of growth and development as Raya and I have come to understand it so far, and it offers a helping hand in crossing the Void between a familiar world and the new places that match your purpose on this planet.

This book describes advanced concepts and methods from the field of Logosynthesis. However, if you're new to the subject, you'll find a brief overview of the Logosynthesis model in the Appendix in Chapter 33. Its most important protocol, the Basic Procedure, is described in Chapter 34. If you get stuck during the exercises in this book, we recommend to run the Basic Procedure to resolve any blocks that show up on your path.

PART I

A PILGRIMAGE

THE ORIGIN OF
LOGOSYNTHESIS®

PART I.
A PILGRIMAGE

Those who do not move do not notice their chains.
— Rosa Luxemburg[10]

A pilgrimage is a journey, often into an unknown or foreign place, where a person seeks new or expanded meaning about themselves, others, nature, or a higher good through experience. It can lead to a personal transformation, after which the pilgrim returns to their daily life.[11]

Human beings rarely understand the meaning of their lives, their destiny, or their mission from the beginning. Most people only gradually discover what suits them, what attracts or repels them, and what they're passionate about through a series of experiences, experiments, and coincidences—and most often by trial and error.

In this section of the book, we outline the conditions for shaping reality we've observed, and we'll invite you on a journey to find your purpose in life.

6   SHAPING THE WORLD
OF FORM

Every thought, action, decision, or feeling
creates an eddy in the interlocking,
interbalancing energy fields of life.
In this interconnected universe,
every improvement we make in our private world
improves the world at large for everyone.
— David Hawkins[12]

6.1 Shaping reality

Shaping reality refers to the ability to access a power beyond the limits of physics, biology, and psychology, to influence your perception and the tangible world. This idea has a rich history, with many creation stories detailing the origins of our current reality. Every culture has its own narrative, explaining how the world came to be, whether in seven days as in the Book of Genesis, or over millions of years of evolution following the Big Bang. Since the dawn of humanity, people have not only told such stories, but have also sought to change the world they inhabit, both as individuals and as cultures. They've done so by either wielding the power of their hands, or by tapping into unseen forces that lie beyond.

When we talk about shaping reality in this book, we believe that you have access to a power beyond the confines of the classical view on physics, biology, and psychology; a power that directly influences your reality. We accept the existence of a transcendent force that not only impacts perceptions, thoughts, emotions, and beliefs, but also influences the objective, tangible world—Essence. Shaping reality is the result of a mysterious synergy between Essence, your Self, and the Matrix; this synergy activates the power of words and builds upon them. Humans are often seen as lacking the innate potential to actively shape reality, except through hard work, sweat, and tears. Anything else is considered magic—either forbidden in one perspective or inexplicable in another.

However, it's worthwhile exploring the idea that humans can shape reality by focusing their intention. Sacred writings and folklore are filled with examples of people achieving the impossible through faith and spiritual experience—what if these stories are true and follow a pattern that we can learn and practice? What if we assume that magic is possible, and miracles do happen? This view allows us to play with new options; it opens a door that has been closed by conventional rationality and provides access to something that has only been available to devout followers of religions.

6.2 Shaping reality for wishes or for purpose

Have you ever wished you could snap your fingers and change a situation when the facts didn't match your expectations? People want to change reality based on their biological, emotional, and mental needs. They want to be happy, healthy, rich, beautiful, famous, and perfect.

However, such an attitude will always create a deficit in the sense that the satisfaction of one need always carries with it the seeds of the another, unfulfilled need. It just doesn't work.

In Jakob and Wilhelm Grimm's story, a poor fisherman catches a magical fish who promises to grant any wish in exchange for its release. The fisherman's wife is excited and makes increasingly extravagant demands, transforming their humble cottage into a grand castle. However, her insatiable desires eventually lead to her downfall. The fish eventually takes back all the granted wishes, leaving the fisherman and his wife destitute and back in their original state. The story serves as a cautionary tale about the dangers of greed and the consequences of limitless desires.[13]

WHY ARE
YOU HERE?

If you bring forth what is within you,
what you bring forth will save you.
If you do not bring forth what is within you,
what you do not bring forth will destroy you.
— The Gospel of Thomas[14]

7.1. You have a mission

Logosynthesis is based on the premise that you and every other person entered life on earth with a mission, a calling, a vocation. This is a unique task given or chosen by your Essence to be realized by your Self in this world. If you are not aware of this meaning, your life may be determined in default by what you expect from the Matrix and by what the Matrix expects from you. Because these mutual expectations are rarely fulfilled, such an attitude often leads to suffering—in the form of fear, shame, guilt, emptiness, doubt, exhaustion, envy, and jealousy.

To end the suffering caused by unfulfilled needs, it is necessary to widen the limited perspective provided by the Matrix. You must answer your calling and accept the tasks that come with it. Once you know why you are here, a fascinating journey begins: Your connections with others intensify, you attract likeminded people with similar interests, and you accomplish your plans more easily. You perceive clear distinctions between your own path and the roles and resources of others. When you become aware of why you're here, you learn to appreciate and respect the diverse perspectives that contribute to a shared human experience—with minimal conflict.

Knowing that your life has meaning makes you more resilient when you are confronted with the mischief and misery that can be triggered by people and circumstances. Awareness of your mission helps you to focus and to find strength. For example: A cancer survivor who believes he or she has a unique role to play in supporting others facing serious illness can find meaning in the face of daunting physical and emotional challenges.

President John F. Kennedy's sister Rosemary was born with mental disabilities. Her condition worsened after a tragic lobotomy. Moved by her sister's struggles, Eunice Kennedy Shriver, another of JFK's sisters, stood up for people like Rosemary. She pushed for new laws to improve the government's care for people with mental disabilities. Eunice's hard work changed both the perception and the practice of how we care for people with such challenges.

7.2 Not every mission is exceptional

Although the news outlets and social media are filled with stories of heroes, champions, leaders, celebrities, and other role models who boast a vast range of exceptional accomplishments, the concept of a unique purpose or meaning does not imply that the meaning of your life must be fantastic, amazing or on public display. Rather, each life has a distinct purpose, which can be found as much in the seemingly ordinary aspects of life as well as the exceptional ones. Embracing humble life can be just as meaningful, satisfying, and impactful as a life in the spotlight. Most meanings are quite normal, somewhat average, and will never make the news.

7.3 Finding your mission statement

The power of words in a mission statement is huge, and it can be an important step on your life path to identify your calling, your X, and to follow it.[15] Grasping its elements and unwrapping your unique X will raise your frequency: Your whole energy system connects to the corresponding receptors in the field around you. As an often unexpected result, the Matrix will support your venture, even if this seems unlikely to you at this moment.

7.4 Your mission statement in words: I. Am. Here. To. X.

Your mission statement contains the following words:
I, Am, Here, To, and X.

I
I in your mission statement represents your Free Self as an expression of your Essence during this time on Earth. This I is in direct contact with your Essence, the origin of your life energy. It differs from the I associated with ego, which is a tool your mind uses to navigate the world around you.

Am
Am is a placeholder for the process of creation itself. I Am is not limited to your current state and identity. It's also an expression of your Essence as a being beyond space and time, and includes what you will be, and what you will be-come: your coming being in the same sense that a seed already contains all the information necessary to become a tree.

Here
Here is the place where you are now, the location that your Essence decided upon as the best possible place to kindle the

light of your mission. It doesn't mean that you must stay here, but before you leave it makes sense to become aware of the qualities of your current location relative to what you have chosen to learn or develop. Here is the corner of the Matrix that's the best fit for your purpose—and you can stay here or start from here before venturing out.

To

To implies that you're here with a reason, a purpose, a meaning, and a mission. Embracing this To means deciding to be here for a reason, even if you haven't found that reason yet.

X

X is a verb that reflects your purpose or mission. It is an ongoing activity that ends only when you leave the Earth. Whenever I ask clients to go back to a time before their conception to find their life mission, they always come up with a single verb: to help, to support, to lead, to serve, to entertain, or to discover. Open your mind and find your X.

7.5 Clearing your mission statement

This exercise helps you to find a pivotal verb that defines your mission, reinforces your intention, activates your Essence, and taps into the resources of the Matrix. Initially, the field strength and frequency of the energy stored in the statement you used in the exercise above may be low. Its energy may be fragmented and scattered because each of its words is packed with different meanings and connotations. Freeing each word from these attachments will allow your energy to flow more freely, clear your intention, and initiate your practice of shaping reality.

Take a moment to read the instructions below, then return

to this point in the text. These instructions will vary based on your familiarity with the Logosynthesis model. The exercise is designed to create a compelling future by concentrating and focusing the energy of your mission statement. When you do this exercise, one of three scenarios may occur:

1. You don't have a clear idea of your mission at this moment in your life. In this case, the X in the exercise is to find your mission. You begin with "I Am Here To Find My Mission," and run the procedure for all seven words of that statement.

2. You're aware of your mission, you have a verb for it, but you don't have any idea what it means in practical terms—yet. You want to use this exercise to resolve the frozen energy related to your intention so that you can establish a better meaning for it, as in "I Am Here To Write."

3. You're aware of your mission, you have a meaningful verb for it, but need more clarity about how to complete a specific concrete task in support of it, such as "I Am Here To Write a Sales Pitch for my Seminar."

When you have chosen your best option for this exercise, make a note of your trust level on a scale of 1-10: 1 means that your trust regarding being able to accomplish the task is very low, 10 is the maximum. Then you apply the three sentences of the Logosynthesis Basic Procedure for every single word of your mission statement, one word at a time, in the following form. You start with I:

1. *I retrieve all my energy bound up in the word "I" in the statement "I Am Here To X," all its representations and everything it represents, and I take it to the right place in my Self.*

2. *I remove all non-me energy related to in the word "I" in the statement "I Am Here To X," all its representations and everything it represents, from all my cells, all my body and from my personal space, and I send it to where it truly belongs.*

3. *I retrieve all my energy bound up in all my reactions to the word "I" in the statement "I Am Here To X," all its representations and everything it represents, and I take it to the right place in my Self.*

Take the time to let each sentence sink in until you feel a shift. Then repeat the procedure for Am, Here, To, and the verb or group of words that names your X. Make notes after each set of sentences.

If you've completed this exercise using a specific task as your X, e.g. I am here to write a sales pitch, act and go for it now. If you intended to gain clarity about your mission, jot down any insights you've uncovered.

To conclude the exercise, say sentence 4 from the Basic Procedure:

4. *I attune all my systems to this new awareness.*

After the exercise, return to the option you chose at the beginning of the exercise. What has changed in your attitude toward the task? Then remember your trust level on the scale 1-10. How has your score on the scale changed?

7.6 A few tips

Your subconscious mind is learning every time that you run either the Logosynthesis Basic Procedure or the elements of an exercise. In the beginning you may need to apply the steps for all five words separately. With growing experience, you can use shortcuts.

Once you have done this exercise a few times, you can apply the Basic Procedure on the full statement instead of on the separate words. E.g., when I'm working on a book, I start my work by running the exercise for *I Am Here To Write Today*. I add "Today" because it creates a space for writing today (and perhaps for walking up a mountain tomorrow).

If you have done the Logosynthesis Basic Procedure a hundred times or more, you can use a shortcut, e.g.:

I run the Logosynthesis Basic Procedure for the word "I"

This shortcut instructs your subconscious mind to perform the procedure without the need to say the full sentences. It's like driving a car: It requires some mechanical practice at first, but after a while you can do it automatically. The effectiveness of the Basic Procedure doesn't seem to diminish when you use the shortcut.

It's important to take your time with any application of the Basic Procedure, including the shortcut. If you feel tired, nauseous, confused, or irritated: Drink water. This usually helps to stabilize your energy system.

Then follow your calling:

> *If something burns your soul with purpose and desire,*
> *it's your duty to be reduced to ashes by it. Any other*
> *form of existence will be yet another dull book in the*
> *library of life.*[16]

8

WHAT DO YOU WANT
TO CREATE?

*The world is a seamless, always self-creating,
self-individuating, and simultaneously self-uniting,
flow that is only truly knowable as it comes to be known.*
— Iain McGilchrist[17]

If you're like most people, you're permanently oscillating between the awareness of your Essence and the realities of the Matrix, in a lifelong unfolding of learning and development. There are times when you can easily connect to your true nature and recognize that you are more than a mind and a body surviving in civilization. At other times, you may struggle to keep up with your to-do list or be overwhelmed by how pedantic the Matrix is.

In diagram 1 on the next page, Essence and the Matrix are drawn as two partly overlapping circles. Essence is shown as a light gray circle on the left, and the Matrix is represented by the dark gray circle on the right. The intersection of both fields has the shape of an almond, a lens, or a flame. This almond, also called *mandorla or vesica piscis*, is an ancient symbol of divine manifestation.[18]

A free flow of energy in this space is the sole condition for manifestation and creation, and it's our purpose in this book to help you to free your life energy in the service of your unique purpose on this planet.

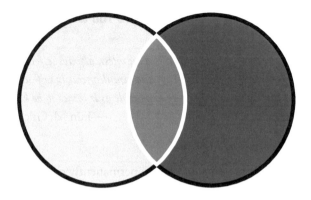

Diagram 1: Essence, the Self, and the Matrix

Your Free Self is the part of the almond where the life energy from your Essence meets the resources of the Matrix. Other parts of the Self are not free, they are *dissociated*. Dissociated parts are frozen in the energy patterns of memories, fantasies, and beliefs, and result from programs and events in the past, especially in early childhood or even before.

Awareness of Essence and the Matrix opens the door to a life that is both creative and sacred, while the fulfillment of physical and emotional needs fades into the background. Logosynthesis protocols and other forms of guided change can gradually restore this flow of your life energy, increasing your freedom and expanding your Free Self.

8.1 What is worth creating?

The Matrix challenges you to review your wishes, needs, and expectations on a regular basis. You may be happy in your mission and with life in general, but some situations are a stalemate: Your relationship with your partner is great, but your mother-in-law is a nightmare—despite extreme patience and your best efforts. You love your job, but your new boss manages to ruin most of your days. You are stuck in the middle of a project and your inspiration has vanished into thin air, leaving you staring blankly at the screen. You are confused, frustrated, lost, or curious.

Many people want to be happy and satisfied. They want to live in a comfortable home and drive a nice car. If you look at research in this field, you'll discover that wealth and comfort only add to happiness until your wealth or income exceeds a certain percentage of the amount you have at your disposal now. Once you've exceeded this financial threshold, additional possessions or resources do not create more happiness—meaning does. Therefore, it is better to strive for the resources and support systems that will best serve your mission.

The most important aspects of your mission are love and meaning. If you're aware of their importance, you'll invest your time, energy, and resources to design your life along those lines. Building loving relationships adds to love in the world, and participating in meaningful activities is more gratifying than fulfilling the needs of body and mind.

A healthy body will serve you when you dedicate your life to a purpose. A certain degree of wealth will allow you to acquire what you need for training and travel, and to buy necessary tools for your activities on your path. When I meet a new client in my practice, I try to understand the experience of love, meaning, health and wealth in their lives, in that order. At the beginning of the therapeutic process, we'll often pay attention to health and wealth. However, this emphasis fades as the client's awareness of love and meaning increases.

8.2 Questions: How do you want to live your life?

How do you want to live your life, regarding:

- *love?*

- *meaning?*

- *health?*

- *wealth?*

Which of these core issues resonates with you the most?

8.3 Clearing your Free Self: Debugging

In our book *Alone to Alive*, we presented the Debugging protocol.[19] It begins with a list of statements that represent an ideal reality for your Free Self. Each statement is a three-word sentence that is cleared of frozen energy patterns to activate the full potential of an aspect of your Self in action. Each statement consists of I, the personal pronoun for your Self, a verb, and an adjective or an adverb. It's not important whether these statements feel true when you start the protocol; however, your Free Self must be able understand them and give them meaning. Examples might be:

- *I am healthy.*

- *I am wealthy.*

- *I am loving.*

- *I am alive.*

- *I have meaning.*

- *I have time.*

- *I am…*

8.4 Clearing your Free Self: an exercise

For this exercise, make a list of at least seven items. Then identify the one that means the most to you and write it down on a new page or in a new document on your word processor. It doesn't matter what being healthy, wealthy, or alive currently means to you in daily life. It's your purpose to strengthen the awareness of your Essence and to reduce and clear any distractions from the Matrix.

After making your list, assess the level of *truth* for each phrase on a scale 0-10: A zero means that the statement is not true at all, that you see the statement as absolute nonsense; and a 10 means that you're fully convinced that it is true. Take the first number that flashes in your mind as you read the statement.

Now, from your list, select the statement that appeals the most to you, the one that you want to bring to life. Is it more important for you to be healthy or wealthy? If it's both, choose the most gratifying one for you in the long run, or the one that you need most for your current task.

Once you've determined the truthfulness of the statement you've chosen, complete a cycle of the three sentences of the Logosynthesis Basic Procedure for each word in that statement.[20] You can use the procedure for any statement you wish to clear from distressing reactions and associations. In the following example, we'll apply the Basic Procedure for the statement, "I am alive."

- Start with a cycle of the Basic Procedure for the word 'I':

1. *I retrieve all my energy, bound up in the word "I" in the statement "I am alive," and I take it to the right place in my Self.*

2. *I remove all non-me energy, related to the word "I" in the statement "I am alive," from all my cells, all my body, and from my personal space, and I send it to where it truly belongs.*

3. *I retrieve all my energy, bound up in all my reactions to the word "I" in the statement "I am alive," and I take it to the right place in my Self.*

- Let each of these sentences sink in until you notice a shift. This can be a feeling of relief or relaxation, a slight change in mood, or a subtle change in the lighting or atmosphere of the room you're in.

- In the next step you run a cycle of the Basic Procedure for the characteristic you want to strengthen; in this case the word *alive* in the sentence *I am alive*:

1. *I retrieve all my energy, bound up in the word "alive" in the statement "I am alive," and I take it to the right place in my Self.*

2. *I remove all non-me energy, related to the word "alive" in the statement "I am alive," from all my cells, all my body, and from my personal space, and I send it to where it truly belongs.*

3. *I retrieve all my energy, bound up in all my reactions to the word "alive" in the statement "I am alive," and I take it to the right place in my Self.*

- Again, let each of these sentences sink in, until you detect a change.

▪ In the next step you forge a connection between the "I" and the characteristic you want to activate and strengthen, with another cycle of the Basic Procedure for the verb form "*am*" in the sentence I am alive:

1. *I retrieve all my energy, bound up in the word "am" in the statement "I am alive," and I take it to the right place in my Self.*

2. *I remove all non-me energy, related to the word "am" in the statement "I am alive," from all my cells, all my body, and from my personal space, and I send it to where it truly belongs.*

3. *I retrieve all my energy, bound up in all my reactions to the word "am" in the statement "I am alive," and I take it to the right place in my Self.*

▪ Now reassess the level of truth for the statement I am alive on a scale 0-10: 0 means not true at all, 10 means that you're fully convinced. Compare this with your previous score.

You can repeat the procedure for any other statement you'd like to debug and strengthen in your life. "I am..." statements serve as a foundation for creating the life you want to move into. From there, you can continue with more specific statements, such as:

▪ *I find love in my life.*

▪ *I learn to dance.*

▪ *I build a house.*

▪ *I move to the city.*

Debugging such statements can lead to unexpected insights and help you gain clarity about both the reality contained within your dreams and the dreams contained within your reality. After completing the debugging protocol, you'll be left with a statement that provides your Self with a clear direction; this is a key requirement for navigating the Void and shaping your new reality within the context of the Matrix you live in.

PART II

THE CONTAINER PRINCIPLE

THE ORIGIN OF
LOGOSYNTHESIS®

PART II.
THE CONTAINER PRINCIPLE

In this section of the book we will introduce you to a simple but insightful concept, that of *container/contained*, which was developed by the English psychoanalyst Wilfred Bion. He developed the idea after World War II, and it has significantly influenced my understanding of human behavior and group dynamics throughout my career. By exploring and applying this principle, you will gain practical knowledge and tools for understanding the environments that you have been a part of in the past, and it will help you to create environments that foster safety, stability, growth, and learning for both yourself and others in the future. In the third section of this book, we'll offer the Move On program to help you explore the options available within your current environment or to move from one container to another.

Bion's container/contained principle focuses on the relationship between an individual (the contained) and the environment (the container) that surrounds them. A container can be a physical space, a biological environment, a group, a place, or even a mindset. For human beings, the containers that surround us influence and shape our thoughts, values, beliefs, emotions, and actions. Understanding this principle enables you to identify factors that have held you back and prevented you from breaking free from limitations. We recommend reading this part in its entirety before you begin to use the Move On program.

In chapter 9, we explore the container concept and describe various types of containers. We discuss the importance of se-

curity and stability for growth and development. A supportive environment enables individuals to feel safe enough to
explore new ideas, to take risks, and to challenge their beliefs.
We provide practical guidance on how to create such an environment, whether it be in a family, a workplace, a classroom,
or within your own mind.

In chapter 10, we examine the undertaking of entering a
new container and the effects it can have on an individual.
Adapting to a new environment is challenging, and understanding how to navigate this transition is crucial for success
and personal growth.

Chapter 11 discusses the concept of growth within a container. Secure families, effective schools, and well-managed
workplaces cultivate an environment that encourages learning, curiosity, and experimentation. This chapter also exam-
ines how to identify resources within a container and the
importance of finding one's niche and role within the support
system. A well-functioning container naturally leads to the
unfolding and fulfillment of one's life mission. However, it's
also possible that you will discover your purpose by exploring
and overcoming the limitations of a container.

Chapter 12 addresses the importance of recognizing when
it's time to leave a container that has served its purpose—i.e.
when you have fulfilled a role or reached a significant milestone. Leaving a safe space and encountering uncertainty
requires courage. We will discuss how courage can grow or
decline based on the challenges faced and highlight the signs
that tell it's time to move on. We will also explore various
criteria for leaving a container or staying in it.

Chapter 13 delves into the concept of courage and its role in facing life's challenges. It highlights the distinction between courage and emotional responses like fear and anxiety.

We discuss how courageous people stay focused on their mission and inspire others. The chapter also emphasizes the importance of reconnecting to your Essence and with the resources of the Matrix to overcome anxiety.

Chapter 14 explores the concept of the Void, a space where your old world is gone but you have not yet reached a safe new environment. We discuss the challenges of embracing the silence, emptiness, grief, and anxiety that can emerge within the Void, as well as the exciting potential it offers for new ideas and perspectives. We touch on the importance of entering the Void with courage.

Chapter 15, the last of this section, introduces Logosynthesis and some of its assumptions that underlie the creation of suitable conditions for being able to shape reality in the Matrix.

Understanding the container principle will help you to create a framework to identify and overcome obstacles and move on in your life.

9 PLACES FOR SAFETY
AND DEVELOPMENT

9.1 What is a container?

The word container comes from two Latin words: *con and tangere*. Taken together, they mean "to hold together," and that's exactly what containers do: You put something into them, and they hold and protect it, keeping disparate elements together. Containers provide a structure and a safety that allows you to grow, learn, and develop. Life takes you through a series of containers: You start in the uterus, move to a cradle, go to school, maybe go to college, then you enter a workplace or start a business. You likely end up in a hospital or hospice bed before being finally laid to rest in a coffin. Containers are everywhere in material form in our daily lives: Bags, boxes, cars, houses, cupboards, kettles, and vases. They become useless the moment that they stop holding and protecting their contents. The fact that we have so many names for them illustrates their significance.

9.2 Containers in biology

Every development in our world starts with an element that requires safe and nurtured growth within a container. This is true for peas in a mange-tout, for a chick in its egg, and for a fetus in the uterus. The container is designed for the sole purpose of creating a secure and nourishing environment for the growth and development of the new being. Some examples from biology include:

- eggs
- nuts, beans, and other seeds

- shells

- a chrysalis

- a nest

- the pouch of a kangaroo or seahorse

- a uterus

Every living being on this planet is conceived—a distinct life force becomes activated in the environment of the Matrix. A flower is pollinated, birds mate, parents have sex: An egg cell meets a sperm, and a new living organism arrives within the boundary of the container that is to provide a safe and flexible space for it to grow. It stays there until it does not need to be contained anymore. A chick breaks the shell of its egg when it has outgrown those confines, and slips under the wings of the mother hen, the next container in its life. Mother hen in turn, is contained within a nest. In a similar way, a human baby leaves the uterus after nine months and is received into its mother's arms—ideally.

9.3 Characteristics of containers

All psychological, social, and cultural systems are containers. They are often embedded within other larger containers, all with the following characteristics:

- They offer a secure space for the development and practice of a specific skill, function, or purpose—the primary task. A school class equips the pupils to reach the next grade; a training institute certifies people with a degree; a nursing home offers protection and care for vulnerable people; a restaurant serves dinner to guests; and a factory buys ingredients or parts, produces things, checks their quality, and then sells them.

■ A container separates those who are contained within it from the wider environment by an outer boundary. This boundary defines who belongs in it and who doesn't. This boundary is defined by such things as a physical structure, a password, a passport, a birth certificate, or a membership card. Boundaries can be hard or soft, permeable or rigid, healthy or not healthy. A healthy boundary will open to receiving resources from the outside world and close to defend itself to harmful influences.

■ Some containers offer exclusive resources that facilitate growth and development over a period of time: You spend a year in each school class, then several years in academia, vocational training, or a workplace. Then you move on—to advance your career, start a business, or retire. Other containers offer different forms of protection: Vulnerable people are taken care of in a nursing home or a hospital. Those who offend society receive a sentence and are sent to a jail cell.

■ In biological, psychological, and social systems, the container itself is changed by the development of the contained. If people provide a leading, caring, or protecting function, they change over the years in the contact with their patients, clients, or charges—the people contained. Relationships mature as interactions become co-created and increasingly nuanced. All parties gather experience and become able to manage larger and more complex tasks, no longer being overwhelmed or exhausted by them.

- Smaller containers are embedded within larger ones. The specific tasks of smaller containers—subsystems—are derived from the primary task of the main container. An enterprise has departments, and each department has its specialties, like production, marketing, purchasing, asset management, and customer service.

9.4 Containers in a wider sense

According to Wilfred Bion, containers are more than physical people or objects; they can also hold something together in a metaphorical or a metaphysical sense. All biological, mental, social, and cultural systems develop within containers. For a smooth development, you as a human being need the following:

- A safe and nurturing environment that provides for your basic needs, such as food, shelter, and protection from harm.

- A supportive community that allows for social and emotional development, such as a family, friends, or other social networks. Families, friends, and neighbors provide the safety needed for a child to learn the skills to survive within and connect to the Matrix.

- Opportunities for exploration, learning, and education. We all need exposure to new experiences, ideas, and concepts that challenge and expand our knowledge and skills. The most common learning environments are provided by your country's education system from kindergarten through to university.

■ A sense of purpose or meaning that provides direction and motivation for your growth and development. On the path to discovering and fulfilling your mission, you will work in organizations that pursue collective goals for their customers, employees, and owners, or for society as a whole. Ideally, these goals also support your mission. If they don't, you will eventually seek out an alternative container.

This is the human condition from the cradle to the grave within the largest container of all—the Matrix.

9.5 Containers hold energy fields in the Matrix

In the Logosynthesis model, everything is energy. Therefore, the container concept is not limited to only physical or social environments. In Logosynthesis, we understand a container as an energy field in the context of the Matrix. Such a container usually comes with a material form, but that's not always the case: Before the pandemic, no one would have thought that schools, universities, or workplaces could function entirely without buildings, and yet they did, with the same dynamics and familiar vibes.

Each container you interact with on your journey is an energy field that leaves an imprint on you. This imprint has a specific frequency and field strength, and it contains information that affects you in many ways. Your energy system holds a representation of every container you've ever been in, and of everything you experienced there—for better or for worse. Conversely, your field also affects the container that contains you.

9.6 Exploring your containers—an exercise

If thinking about life as a series of containers is a new concept for you, the following exercise will help you gain more clarity:

1. Find a quiet time and space in your day.

2. Take your journal or open a new document on your laptop.

3. Think about your life and list all the containers you recognize in random order.

4. Once it becomes difficult for you to think of any new ones, put them in chronological order and choose one—from the present or the past.

5. Answer the following questions and write down your responses:

- *What is the name of this container?*
- *How long have you been in it?*
- *How old were you during this time?*
- *How did this container meet your needs?*
- *What did you learn while you were there?*
- *What resources were available for you in this container?*
- *Who or what was/is holding this container and who or what was/is responsible for it?*

Write down your answers as a little story and save it for Part III where you'll be able to move on from limiting effects or situations.

9.7 Containers under stress

Each container needs to have an outer boundary. This boundary protects the contained subjects from external hazards and allows resources to enter. Each container also needs an authority: a person, or a group of people, or an organizational structure that maintains that boundary and provides resources in the service of security and development. If this authority is a person, it may be a parent, teacher, instructor, doctor, or leader. If it's a group of people or a structure, it may be a management team, a board, a council, or a government with different branches and hierarchical levels.

If a container fulfills its function, the subject held in it will grow until they don't need it anymore. However, a container may fail in different ways:

▪ Violation of the outer boundary: The responsible authority is not strong enough to defend the system against danger from the outside world. This is the case when children experience bullying, it happens when a virus attacks a cell, when a business is involved in an unfriendly takeover, or when a country is invaded in an act of war.

▪ Authority figures or structures fail to fulfill their roles: The container boundary may hold, but the danger or lack comes from within. The subject in the container is not safe because their needs are not met, or they do not receive necessary resources.

If a container is under stress, it is often due to a combination of these two aspects. Some stresses are obvious, such as an accident, an illness, or a death in the family. In time, the container may adjust; it recovers and continues with its purpose. How well it adjusts depends on the quality of its resources and the health of its relationships. A wealthy, well-functioning family may manage death, divorce, and stressful life events more easily than a family with less wealth, a minimal support system, and a dysfunctional dynamic.

At other times, stress factors are invisible or only affect single individuals. Domestic abuse, workplace bullying, or discrimination fall into this category. Such stress will arrest growth and development, causing pain long after someone has left the container.

Occasionally, stress can affect everyone, like an earthquake or other natural disaster, or when an organization breaks down, such as when a church disbands after the blatant hypocrisy of a once-respected minister is exposed.

Internal and external damage and conflict undermine security and hinder growth. An extremely high stress level may cause a container to implode or explode, causing extreme pain and distress.

Similar patterns can be seen in the overall workings of the Matrix when global events generate extensive uncertainty. This is evident in the occurrence and effects of the pandemic, the wars in Europe and the Middle East, and the threat of climate change.

For vulnerable people, these factors—transgression of the outer boundary of a container, and the inadequate functioning of an authority—can lead to traumatic experiences and stress disorders. If you identified strong stressors in the exercise above, you may still be experiencing the painful and limiting effects from that time in your life.

9.8 From contained to containing

During healthy development, there will come a time when you evolve from needing to be contained, to taking responsibility for others and becoming an authority yourself. In the middle to later stages of life, people tend to create or maintain holding environments for others. They provide care and support—as parents, grandparents, managers, teachers, leaders, entrepreneurs, legal or military officers, coaches, consultants, and psychotherapists. Most adults have multiple roles and responsibilities that provide these functions.

Shifting from contained to containing can take different forms: You might take on a new role that you have sought or strived for, or such a role may be presented to you by the Matrix. For the new role, you'll need to acquire additional competence and develop an attitude that lives and expresses your authority. During their realignment, people need support, and it's not surprising that they seek coaching or counseling to help them adapt to their new position. The nature of necessary support depends on which corner of the Matrix you find yourself in. If it's not offered, you're in for a big challenge.

Eventually, in your most senior years, after you have gradually shed your responsibilities and roles, you may again be contained in the holding environment of a hospital or nursing home.

9.9 Two stories

Valentina

Valentina was born in a small town to a loving family that provided her with a safe and nurturing environment. Her childhood was full of happiness and warmth, as her parents ensured that her needs were met. Valentina felt safe and loved in her family.

As she grew older, Valentina found good people in her community of family, friends, and social networks that supported her social and emotional development. Her natural intelligence and curiosity led her to explore new experiences and ideas, which challenged and expanded her knowledge and skills.

During her teenage years, Valentina met a good looking and kind-hearted young man named Lucas. They became life partners and created a positive home environment where both could flourish. As they navigated the ups and downs of life, they found purpose and meaning together, further cementing their bond.

It wasn't long before Valentina and Lucas became parents, welcoming Madlaina into the world. For Valentina, motherhood was a beautiful experience, a new container for her growth and development. She offered the same nurturing care she had experienced to her child, instilling a deep sense of security and well-being.

Years passed, and Valentina became a loving grandmother. Valentina and Lucas' home became a haven of joy for their grandchildren, who would visit, play, talk and bake, all the while learning from their wisdom.

As Valentina grew older, she reflected on her life and the various containers she had experienced. Each stage—childhood, partnership, motherhood, and older age—had offered unique opportunities for growth, development, and maturation. Through it all, she recognized the importance of both experiencing and providing a supportive environment for herself and the people around her.

Valentina's story illustrates the necessary conditions for healthy growth throughout one's life. Recognizing these conditions allows you to better understand your own needs and those of others. When you have such an understanding, you access the power to create environments that foster well-being and fulfillment at any stage. You will also be able to recognize where and why particular containers are not working as well as they might. This knowledge equips you to implement strategies and interventions that will restore safety and balance. You will be able to lead effectively, and with a compassionate attitude.

Felix

Felix's story is different from Valentina's. He grew up in a poor and rundown town. Born into a fractured family, he experienced a childhood devoid of safety and nurture. He rarely saw his father, and his mother worked long hours trying to make ends meet, but sadly fell short in providing his basic needs for food, shelter, and protection, leaving him vulnerable and insecure.

As he grew older, Felix longed for the supportive community that he saw others enjoying. Unfortunately, his social and emotional development suffered due to a lack of meaningful connection with his family, friends, or other social networks. There was barely any time and money for learning and exploration, and his knowledge and skills remained stunted, preventing him from growing and evolving as his classmates did.

As a young adult, Felix entered a tumultuous relationship with Charlotte. Their connection was volatile and uncertain, and it didn't have a clear purpose or direction. Felix yearned for a sense of meaning and significance, but these things remained elusive, exacerbating the cycles of discontent and frustration.

As the years went by, Felix and Charlotte unexpectedly became the parents of Jakob. Their already unsteady world was shaken. Like Felix and Charlotte, Jakob also struggled to find security and happiness. Felix was unable to break the pattern of limitation set in place by his own upbringing and therefore handed it down to his son.

Time went on, and Felix faced the challenges of aging. His life had been marked by a series of losses and unfulfilled needs, wishes, and desires. His childhood, partnership, parenthood, and now old age had been difficult. Each stage had been marred by missed opportunities for growth and development, leaving him unfulfilled and alone.

Felix's story shows what can happen when necessary conditions are not met. The consequences can be far-reaching and felt deeply for a long time. These effects impact not only one's own well-being but also that of future generations.

Valentina and Felix don't really exist, and no one suffered while writing these accounts, but you may recognize aspects of their stories in your own life. Living in the Matrix brings a mix of experiences and events that either support you on your path or present a harsh reality.

You have the advantage of being able to use the Logosynthesis model to identify, understand, and resolve life's vicissitudes. It provides interventions that will help you to overcome limitations that you have acquired due to unmet needs and adverse experiences. These are not your fault, and you can recover.

9.10 Roles within containers

Your Free Self is in a constant dance between the awareness of your mission from Essence and the rules and requirements of the Matrix. You need to be contained to be able to learn and practice, and after you have reached mastery in a field, you become a container for others while they learn and practice.

As soon as you arrive on Earth, you're assigned some roles. A role is a function that you either willingly assume or that is assigned to you in the context of a particular environment. As a human, you play different roles within your family than you do when you are out in society, just like an actor who plays one character in a drama and another in a comedy. All your roles are embedded in containers that provide an environment where you hold the space for someone else, or where someone else takes care of you. You can even do both in the same container if you are in middle management or if you are a teacher reporting to the principal.

Skilled, competent adults exercise more *containing* roles as family members or professionals in their field of competence. People who are young, old, ill, vulnerable, or criminal, have roles in which they need to be contained—in homes, schools, hospitals, or prisons. Any role that you have in society comes with two key questions:

1. *What is expected from you in this role?*

The expectations that come with a role have nothing to do with you as a person. They are derived from the task that needs to be fulfilled, and the Matrix has a set of expectations around what is required. In organizations, these are openly specified as job descriptions. Expectations are a set of hidden assumptions about your thoughts, emotions, and behavior when you enter the field of a team or organization. In families and informal groups, such expectations are hidden in the collective energy field of the group, and you notice them only when you transgress a boundary that you were not aware of.

2. *What do you expect from this role?*

Some people play their roles exactly according to the rules and codes prescribed by the Matrix. Others consider specified rules as an annoying evil that they prefer to ignore whenever possible. Many conflicts between people are role conflicts: The expectation of the environment doesn't match the person's perception or performance of the required attitude, tasks and behavior. Their best efforts may be effective, yet still not tick the boxes of the container or those of a particular colleague—and conflict then ensues between requirements, interpretations, and expectations.

It took me years to realize that explicit agreements on rules and roles are necessary to run an organization: I had my own ideas about how the work should be done. To my surprise, my boss consistently communicated his expectations with unwavering clarity. My reluctance to embrace these rules ultimately led me to leave the job and launch my own business. Only after hiring my own team and founding my first institute did I truly grasp the wisdom behind my former boss's approach.

9.11 Containers are energy patterns

From the viewpoint of Logosynthesis, everything in the universe is energy vibrating at different frequencies, ranging from (seemingly) solid matter to the highest levels of divine consciousness. To be more precise, we could say: Matter, energy, information, and consciousness are deeply interrelated and are all part of the same web. One cannot exist without the others.[21] In this frame of reference, a container is a complex energy pattern, a structure that is focusing the intentions of individuals and groups on a common task: This can include things like developing an idea, offering a service, manufacturing a product, or anything else for which the world is ready.

Every container exists within other complex energy fields: Containers are nested within each other, or they overlap. Every container consists of patterned information and offers conditions for the survival and development of those contained within it—from the cradle to the coffin. Children are ideally raised in a family, that family belongs to a community, that community is part of a city, and that city is part of a country. Each of these containers is associated with a frame of reference filled with beliefs about gender, race, class, money, education, work, sex, religion, politics, and other people. Every family field holds its own beliefs—specific to the family system and its place within the Matrix.

Of course, not everyone lives in a traditional family unit; monks live as a community in a monastery as members of an order. Disadvantaged children are taken into the care system and sadly often experience constant movement between temporary containers. Other children attend boarding school, live in orphanages, or drop out from society. Soldiers are designated a barracks, the sick to hospitals, the elderly to retirement or nursing homes, criminals to prisons, and homeless people to shelters.

Understanding containers in terms of energy patterns that exist within the context of the Matrix allows you to influence them: If a particular field in the environment supports your mission, Logosynthesis work can provide access to it. If a field or pattern of belief stands in your way, Logosynthesis methods can help you to remove the obstacle, to change your relationship to it, or leave it. The power of words activates the energy of your Essence to address and dissolve these invisible frozen patterns and to create new ones.

When something new is intended to become reality, what is necessary at the Matrix level to make it happen? Elon Musk's example illustrates this point. His company, Tesla, was founded on the belief that electric cars could help reduce carbon dioxide levels in the atmosphere. This innovative idea led to the development of a wide range of electric vehicles, each designed with sustainability in mind. To support these vehicles, Musk also installed a charging infrastructure.

Musk's impact on the automotive industry has been significant, causing other companies to rethink their approach to vehicle production. Most are now developing and manufacturing their own electric vehicles, recognizing the increasing demand for sustainable transportation options, and the need to remain competitive. Thus, the industry can help to reduce pollution and promote sustainable practices for future generations, even though the pollution caused by battery production is still an element of legitimate criticism.

9.12 The Matrix is a container

As we wrote in *Alone to Alive*, your Free Self emerges at the interface of Essence and the Matrix. Its growth and development take place in the largest container of your life: the Matrix.

The Matrix serves as a global container for life on Earth, encompassing everything the world offers its inhabitants. Its complexity is immense, and no person, living or deceased, will ever be able to fully understand it. In *Alone to Alive*, we discussed how people simplify this complexity with the help of beliefs, and how these beliefs either support or hinder their growth. If a belief restricts growth, you can neutralize or resolve it and move forward with awareness and ease.

9.13 Exercise: Explore your fields

Here are a series of questions, which we will repeat in different forms in the following chapters. Take a few minutes to explore your answers and to make some notes in response to them. The first one is:

- *What are the most important containers or fields in your life? A love relationship? Your family? Your circle of friends? Your job? An organization, such as a company, a sports club, or church?*

Now zoom in on the most important of these containers or fields and answer the following questions:

- *What are the functions or tasks of this field in your life?*

- *Which roles do you have in this field?*

- *Which of these roles are receiving roles?*

- *Which of these roles are providing roles?*

- *Which resources do you receive and utilize from this field?*

- *Which of your resources do you offer to this field?*

- *Do expectations from the field match with yours?*

You can repeat this exercise for each of the containers you have identified. Keep your answers to the questions ready for use later in Part III.

9.14 Chloe, part 1: exploring containers

Chloe, one of our trainees who serves as a social worker in a poor neighborhood, used the above exercise to reflect on the fields and containers in her life. She lives alone, and she realized that her job was a significant container. She focused on it to answer the same questions that you have just explored.

- She identified the function of her job as helping to uplift and empower the community she is assigned to. She also recognized that her role as a case manager and advocate for her clients combined a mix of both receiving and providing roles.

- In her role, Chloe receives resources such as a steady income and a supportive work environment. She offers her skills, knowledge, and compassion to her clients. She identified the expectation that her efforts would positively impact the lives of her clients in a variety of ways, and she noted that her supervisors expected her to fulfill her duties and responsibilities based on the documented legal standards of a social worker.

- Chloe found that her own expectations were consistent with her job description, and she had already worked to resolve some minor conflicts about role interpretation and expectations that she had with her boss. However, she rated her level of distress about being able to fulfill her roles in the field at 7 out of 10. She attributed this to the emotional burden of working with multiple clients struggling with generational poverty and trauma. This will be the subject of her future supervision sessions.

- Through this exercise, Chloe realized that her job was a valuable field in her life. She was able to identify areas of strength and areas for potential growth and self-care. She was able to use this understanding to continue to serve her community, while also improving the quality of her self-care and identifying issues that may require further work.

9.15 Lily, part 1: a quest for growth and support

Lily is an artist. She feels deeply connected to her family, her rural town, and the two main communities of which she is a part: her creative group, The Collective, and her online personal growth community. She has been part of The Collective for many years and this group has been vital for sharing and promoting artwork, floating ideas, and sparking inspiration. It also provides her with significant financial opportunities.

▪ In this community, Lily both gives and receives. She earns recognition and respect, she has many opportunities to form collaborative partnerships, to earn income, and to receive valuable feedback. She offers her expertise, her passion, encouragement, and resources to her fellow artists. However, Lily's expectations don't always match the expectations of the field, and this causes her repeated episodes of distress, which show up as physical symptoms and fear of the future.

▪ Lily had hoped that her unique mixed media series, Whispers of Light, would receive much more recognition than it did. She had worked hard, and the process had been long. The feedback from her peers had been good; and yet the exhibition hadn't had the impact or the reach she had hoped for. She felt unfulfilled and depressed. The Collective expects her to actively participate and to continue creating art, but Lily secretly struggles with the interpretations and high expectations of the art world. She feels like a rebel and struggles with complex emotions stemming from her unfulfilled desires.

▪ As she enters mature adulthood, Lily reflects on the years she hasn't been able to fully embrace her artistic identity and feels sadness and a sense of loss. She is also aware of the pressures of time. Nevertheless, she is determined to keep moving forward in her artistic endeavors with The Collective, seeking a balance between giving and receiving, while yearning for personal growth and fulfillment. Lily continues to cope with the various expectations that come from the creative field and realizes the importance of finding her own path regarding artistic success.

When you enter a new container as the next step in your development, you're vulnerable. During your stay, you learn why the container exists, how to access its resources, and how to acquire the skills and power that allow you to eventually leave it.

10.1 Arriving in a new container or field

The most important function of a new container is to provide safety. If you do not feel safe, you will not be able to learn. Once you're comfortable, you will begin to relax and to trust. Trust allows you to connect or to reconnect with your Essence and to the resources within the new field. When you trust, you become curious and begin to explore, and when you feel at home, you can dedicate your time and energy to the reason why you're in this particular container and not another.

At this moment, you're not worrying about the future. You know this is the right spot for you, and you don't have to choose: The ideas and activities you experience are dictated by the container's purpose. Whether you're playing a musical instrument or getting golf lessons from a pro, you're always learning and ready for the next challenge when the time comes.

10.2 What can go wrong?

When you enter a new environment, all sorts of things can go wrong:

- You don't feel safe or welcome. The new environment isn't willing or able to offer you a space, answer your questions, or meet your needs. Anxiety increases while trust decreases, and you feel guilty, ashamed, or sad, eventually becoming depressed.

- You're overwhelmed by the expectations of your role in the new environment. The people there expect someone who already knows the history, the rules, and the implicit patterns of the container—while you don't have a clue what those are yet.

- The new container doesn't respect your knowledge, skills, and experience. They don't accept what you offer, and you get bored.

If expectations don't match, both sides will be frustrated.

10.3 Exercise: exploring fields

Remember the exercise from the previous chapter, where you explored the current fields in your life. Now explore and write down the answers to the following questions:

- *Which is your most important source of safety and comfort?*

- *Which is the most important field for your personal and spiritual development at this stage of your life?*

- *Which role(s) do you play in this field?*

- *Which role(s) are you expected to play in this field?*

- *Which roles do you want to play in this field?*

- *Which roles do you want to change or leave?*

- *Which emotions do you feel in your current environment?*

10.4 Chloe, part 2: meeting limits

Chloe, our social worker, answered the above questions as follows:

▪ The most important source of safety and comfort at this stage of her life is her job as a social worker. It provides her with a sense of purpose, stability, and financial security.

▪ The most important field for her personal and spiritual development is her involvement in a local community group where the focus is on helping families in need. She finds meaning and fulfillment in this work, as well as deeper personal connections with volunteers in the group, some of whom she has known for many years. These activities align with her personal values and, as a group, they have a lot of fun.

▪ For Chloe, being in the role of a supportive and compassionate advocate for the families she works with matches her mission. She experiences moderate distress when facing challenging situations or when dealing with too much bureaucracy and paperwork.

▪ She is expected to play the role of a knowledgeable and experienced professional who can provide solutions and guidance to the families she serves. She feels moderate distress when facing high caseloads or when dealing with particularly complex family dynamics.

▪ Chloe wants her workplace to be a supportive and collaborative environment that values her contributions and helps her grow as a professional. While some of these expectations are fulfilled, she sometimes feels overwhelmed and undervalued. She has occasionally considered looking for a new role, but not too seriously. She imagines that leaving her current job would be emotional for everyone involved and she expects to feel some anxiety at the prospect of starting over in a different organization.

■ In her current environment, Chloe feels compassion, empathy, and gratitude towards the families she serves. She also experiences occasional frustration and sadness when dealing with difficult cases or when an intervention is unsuccessful.

10.5 Lily, part 2: struggles and aspiration

■ At this stage in her life, Lily's partner, Tom, is her main source of safety and comfort. He supports her both emotionally and financially and has significantly contributed to her artistic development over the years. However, Lily finds herself yearning for a deeper, perhaps spiritual connection with others, feeling that a sense of oneness is somehow missing. This aspect is crucial for her personal and spiritual development at this time.

■ Lily dreams of becoming a teacher and mentor, sharing her knowledge and experience in the commercial art world. She fondly recalls her past experiences teaching advanced art classes and supporting less experienced artists, but technology's rapid evolution has made it challenging for her to keep up. This frustration, and the inability to fulfill her desired role causes her considerable distress.

■ In her artistic community, Lily is unsure of the specific roles she is expected to play. She is overwhelmed and exhausted by the complexity of her world; it's as if she's constantly running after elusive opportunities that slip through her fingers. This causes her even more distress. Despite her best efforts, Lily's expectations for recognition and prestigious opportunities are frustrated and remain unfulfilled. She has a good social and professional network and expends a lot of energy maintaining it. She continues to navigate her challenges in the art world, hoping to find a unique position and role where she can make the meaningful impact she dreams of.

11   TIME TO BE:
LIVING IN A CONTAINER

*At the end of the day or week or month what really matters
is that you and your loved ones are safe und well,
you have done your best
and are grateful for being who you are
and touching the world with your presence.*
— Rajesh Goyal[22]

11.1 When a container resonates

Professionals in guided change, like coaches, counselors, or psychotherapists are rarely needed when a person is well-contained in the Matrix. Families that offer sufficient security and space to grow up don't need a family therapist; a school that adequately protects pupils and challenges them at the correct level of development doesn't need a school social worker, and a workplace that is well-managed, welcoming to new employees, with clearcut job descriptions and a constructive team culture, doesn't need to create opportunities for extra coaching. In general, a supportive environment can help individuals thrive and grow without the need for additional support from professionals.

Once you've overcome the obstacles associated with entering a container, a relatively peaceful state follows. You have found your place in a family, a school class, or a team, and your skills, knowledge, and experience are steadily growing. You look back with satisfaction, and you look ahead with curiosity. The expectations from the outside world match your intention. You've found your niche in a role that fits your mission in the Matrix at this stage of your life, and you're quite happy.

There is a unique comfort to be found in these familiar spaces. It's similar to the feeling of slipping into a well-worn pair of shoes; there is an understanding of their form, a confidence in their support and comfort, and a trust in their capacity to aid your journey. Such a familiar haven offers you an environment you know well, roles you've grown into, and a community that acknowledges and values your contributions. This familiarity, along with the sense of belonging it fosters, can create a deep-seated security that makes staying the easy and obvious choice.

Such a state of undisturbed happiness can last from several months to many years. You can deal with issues that arise through your own competence, or you can get help from those responsible for the environment holding you. You gather experience by practice and repetition. The level of tension between support and challenge suits you well, and you usually enjoy the interchange.

These periods may not seem spectacular, and many people realize only in hindsight how happy they were during these times. Of course, there will be exceptions in which an individual may need additional support or training, especially when arriving or leaving a container, and we'll discuss this further in the next section.

Sadly, or fortunately, no container is available forever. Children leave home, a career step or a new partner leads to a move out of town, contracts are terminated by employers or retirement, and relationships end with divorce or death. If your current container allows for security and growth, you will feel comfortable and be happy to stay there. If the container is not safe or you have reached the limits of its possible expansion, it may be a relief to go. How long you stay in each container depends on your choices. You decide every day whether to stay or go in a friendship, a marriage, or a job, based on both internal and external factors.

11.2 When a container doesn't resonate

Containers are environments in which you ideally find your place, grow, mature, and contribute to the world in some way. However, life doesn't always present us with ideal situations. Sh*t happens. A container may not feel right; you feel like an outsider looking in or you feel alone despite your best efforts to connect. You do not and cannot resonate with this place any longer.

Ill-fitting containers can appear at any life stage. They can trigger intense feelings of alienation, especially during the beginning or end of your stay. If you have little or no choice about being there, or if your survival depends on it, staying in such an environment can be painful or even destructive.

Paradoxically, such a container can provide the stability people need in their current life. Even if they have nothing to lose but their chains, the pain of taking the risk to depart towards the unknown may feel more daunting than staying in a miserable or even dangerous situation that is stable over time. Women and children may live in the same home as their abuser for years. Employees stay in a toxic workplace because they need the money. A drug addict belongs to a scene in a far corner of the Matrix that offers safety and helps find their dealer.

The effects of staying in such limiting containers can be profound. It's like living in a house where the walls don't echo your laughter or absorb your tears—a place where you exist, but do not live. The constant dissonance can erode your self-confidence and heighten your stress levels, leading to feelings of loneliness, despair or even trauma.

In normal life, you're living in multiple containers of which some might support your development and others might hinder it. If a child is unhappy at home, they can enjoy going to school, and the converse is also sometimes true. A happy home can compensate for a distressing workplace. Containers may also collide and increase the stress level in both. Taking care of elderly parents while also having young children can be extremely demanding.

We're not yet exploring solutions or escape routes. Instead, we're shedding light on a common, yet little discussed reality of life. A regular self-check may be the first step in acknowledging uncomfortable truths about your choices and making changes that align with your true intentions and purpose. This ongoing introspection plays a critical role in your journey and will guide you towards new choices. Discomfort and uncertainty are often signals of transformation.

It takes courage to face the truth; it is easier to ignore the facts or to dissociate from them, continuing with the same old, same old—even though it's painful.

Are you OK as you are, do you need to change your current situation, or is it time to search for a space where you can truly thrive?

11.3 Explore your containers

Return to the list of containers you made earlier:

▪ *Which containers make you feel comfortable and confident?*

▪ *Which containers trigger distress?*

▪ *Are there any containers that elicit high distress and low trust? Describe your thoughts and beliefs about this container. Save these notes for part III.*

▪ *Which resources are underutilized within existing containers? Explore how these resources may support you in your current role(s).*

11.4 Chloe, part 3: time for a change

Chloe has always experienced a sense of fulfillment as a social worker in an underprivileged area. However, her emotionally strenuous job is often demanding and leaves her overwhelmed and frustrated. The persistent societal and cultural issues impacting her community, combined with bureaucratic hurdles and long working hours, affect her professional life. Her motivation and empathy towards her clients are dwindling.

▪ Chloe finds herself emotionally and physically exhausted, and this affects the quality of her work with clients. Her routine supervision appointments are vital; they offer the space and guidance she needs to solve problems and devise strategies to navigate the complexities of her vocation.

▪ Lately, Chloe has come to recognize that she has gleaned all the knowledge and experience she needs from this role, there is nothing new that comes her way anymore, and she is even a little bored. She realizes that it might be time to acknowledge these internal alarm signals and seriously consider whether she would benefit from evolving within her current environment or seeking a new one altogether.

▪ After considerable introspection and discussion with her family, and with a sense of completion, Chloe decides that it's time for a new and next step.

11.5 Lily, part 3: emotional crossroads

Lily, the artist, regularly travels for several hours from her home in rural Illinois to her studio in the city of Chicago. She finds solace and support in her partner, Tom. He cheers her on and nurtures her artistic ambitions. However, she feels trapped in a cultural backwater, and craves the excitement and opportunities of the Chicago art scene. Her therapy with a Logosynthesis professional has been transformative, but she's currently at a crossroads, struggling to progress in her sessions.

▪ Lily dreams of having commercial gallery representation in Chicago but her goals are out of reach due to her lack of the right connections and credentials. She is in a dilemma: She appreciates the comfort and security of her life with Tom, and she also wants to live her artist life Chicago without him. Her emotions around creativity are a mix of peace, joy, and curiosity, but she is very aware of the gnawing shame, guilt, and sadness when she thinks of Tom and her home.

▪ Feeling somewhat superior to her local rural art community, and angered by the limited opportunities there, she resents the three-hour travel time it takes to attend events in Chicago. Her desire for the city's energy is palpable, but her love and loyalty to Tom, as well as the financial constraints, hold her back. Caught between two worlds, Lily struggles to find her way between her head and her heart.

TIME TO GO:
LEAVING A CONTAINER

Courage is the most important
of all the virtues because without courage,
you can't practice any other virtue consistently.
— Maya Angelou[23]

12.1 Mission accomplished

Once a role or a container has served its purpose in providing safety and supporting your development towards a certain milestone or goal, you must move on. Leaving a safe space can be painful and takes courage. You may change roles or leave a container because you've outgrown it, or because the container no longer protects you from external stressors. The people within the container may not be able to provide you with the necessary protection for various reasons:

■ They don't have the power to protect or support, as in situations of war and disaster. In these circumstances, external forces overwhelm the container, making safety impossible.

■ They don't live up to their responsibilities, as seen in cases of child neglect and abuse. In such instances, those who should have protected and nurtured failed to fulfill their roles, causing harm to those who relied on them.

■ They lack the necessary resources. Caregivers or authority figures may wish to support and help, but they can be unable to, due to insufficient means or reserves.

Sometimes your growth and development can be revived by changing your roles within an existing container. After working for six years in pulmonary rehabilitation as a psychologist and a psychotherapist, I had become competent in the field, but felt bored, and started to look around for a new job. The director of the hospital had observed me doing this for a while. He didn't want to lose my competence, and when a new organizational structure was installed, he offered me a role as the manager of the hospital's adult department. That position required me to contain a team and kept me busy for another six years. Then it was time to leave the hospital altogether and start my own business.

When you change roles or containers, you enter a place of uncertainty, the Land of Don't Know, as Joan Borysenko calls it. In unfamiliar territory, previous problem-solving strategies may not be effective:[24]

> *Whether you've left to get a new job, or you've left a relationship, or you're just trying to leave behind a belief system (…) you have to enter for a while into that Land of Don't Know: Don't know what I know, don't know where I'm going, and that's a very frightening place for most people. Don't Know is a fascinating place, a place where we lay fallow for a while until something new comes. It's the place where we have died to who we were, but not have been born to what we might be.*

In this unfamiliar world, you need courage—the courage to navigate a Void. Your courage will have grown if the previous container fulfilled its purpose. Your courage will have waned if the circumstances overwhelmed your potential to cope with them. You may be left feeling drained, disoriented, or feeling ill-equipped to cope with the upcoming new situation: facing a job loss, handling a health crisis, or taking an honest look at a difficult relationship. You can't run away, and you can't fight either, you're stuck, unable to think or to act.

The decision to stay in a container or to leave it often results from factors that are deeply intertwined with your beliefs and emotions but can also be influenced by events in the outside world. In this complex fusion, things eventually come to a head, as one last straw breaks the camel's back, and suddenly the container disintegrates. At other times, a mosaic of factors that accumulate over a considerable time contribute to a slow and eventual decision.

At times, the decision isn't yours to make, and you are compelled to remain in a container that has become more like a confined space than a nurturing environment. You may stay in a job for financial security, a family dynamic you were been born into, a city you've moved to for reasons beyond your control, or a relationship in which you're trying to meet someone else's needs rather than your own.

As you're nearing the end of your time in a container or a role, you may notice some changes. You recognize that you can't stay there for much longer, you notice a discomfort and a restlessness that weren't there before, and you observe your relationships becoming more strained and less tolerant. You also catch glimpses of the next part of your journey in an unexpected conversation, a social media message, or a poster on the street, and recognize in a flash: "Yes! That's it!"

This new chapter of your life could entail attending university, a career change, or leaving the practice green to fully immerse yourself in a game of golf. If you are moving towards retirement, you must weave a narrative for your future that includes gradually stepping away from your work and embracing new relationships, interests, and activities that enrich your life. Usually, before leaving a container, you must meet specific requirements:

- You need roughly nine months in utero to breathe on your own.

- Six years of High School are necessary to acquire basic skills and to prepare you for higher levels.

- Your graduation from high school or university marks the end of your formal education.

- You receive a license to provide a service after finishing post-graduate training.

- You need to reach a certain age to officially retire.

The end of your stay in a holding environment often comes with a milestone marking the transition. Receiving the certificate of an education, a wedding ceremony, the baptism of a child, or the farewell dinner offered by your employer are rituals that signify key life events: The end of one chapter and the beginning of another. It can be both exciting and daunting as you adapt to the changes. There is always an aspect of anticipation and an aspect of grief—the two sides of the coin of transition. For a transition to become a transformation, it is crucial to acknowledge both sides.

12.2 Exploring fields

Remember your list of fields from the exercises in the previous chapters and explore the following questions, adding your answers to the previous ones:

■ *Which fields or roles do you want to stay in at this stage in your life?*

■ *Which fields or roles do you want to change?*

■ *Which fields or roles do you want to leave?*

12.3 Chloe, part 4: discovering opportunities

After answering the questions above, Chloe realizes that her job as a social worker is causing her too much distress. Also, this job doesn't align with her ideas about continuing development. She has considered finding a new position before and knows that the stress will only cease with a decision. It's time to explore options that match her strengths and her passions, even though she will miss her colleagues and clients. After some research, she identifies several options:

■ One is to pursue a career in community organizing. This option would allow her to work with individuals and groups to effect change on a larger scale. The prospect of mobilizing communities around important issues and advocating for social justice is exciting.

■ Another option is to become a therapist, specializing in trauma and grief counseling. Chloe has always been drawn to helping people with disturbing experiences, and her background in social work would be an asset in this field.

- A third option is a career in policy advocacy or research, utilizing her knowledge and experience to initiate systemic change at a higher level. This would involve working with organizations or think tanks to develop and implement policies that address the root causes of poverty and inequality.

As she weighs her options, Chloe decides to conduct some informational interviews and job shadowing to gain a better understanding of each field before making a final decision. Though leaving her current job is a major and a difficult decision, Chloe is excited about her future. She is ready to enter the Land of Don't Know.

12.4 Lily, part 4: taking stock

In her journey so far, Lily has relied on her partner, Tom, for support and encouragement. However, she now struggles to find excitement in the stability he offers. Lily's personal growth is rooted in her Logosynthesis psychotherapy, which has helped her regain her sense of Self after a difficult upbringing. When she was younger, Tom had been her rock; over the years, as she has healed her wounds and grown as a person, she doesn't need Tom in the same way anymore. Although she is willing to adapt and be flexible in the relationship, he is not. This has led to tension and conflict in recent months.

- Feeling most alive in Chicago, Lily finds it challenging to balance her life between the green fields of rural Illinois and the city buzz of the Chicago Art Collective. The idea of public recognition and fame is appealing to her. However, her lack of an MFA degree and the right connections in the art world cause her immense distress.

- Despite her emotional struggles, Lily finds joy and peace when working in her studio with color and texture, she is very inspired by nature and finds solace in observing natural forms, then recreating them in her own unique way. She yearns for the environment and opportunities in Chicago.

- Lily's therapy continues to help her explore the complex web of emotions, aspirations, and challenges she experiences as she strives to find her place in the art world and overcome personal obstacles.

COURAGE MEETS
THE VOID

As you go the way of life,
you will see a great chasm. Jump.
It is not as far as you think.
— A Native American Chief to a teen at the
time of his initiation.[25]

13.1 What is courage?

Courage is not an emotion—it's a state in which you have
the power to undertake something that you recognize as
difficult or daunting; it's the mental or moral strength to
venture, and persevere.[26] Courage is bravery, the quality of
mind or spirit that enables you to face distress, danger, and
hardship.[27]

Many people become trapped by inertia when they must
leave the safety and comfort of a familiar world, often struggling with embracing the uncertainties and potential risks of
the Land of Don't Know. They need courage because deep
change is rarely without pain.

Courage implies that you don't know the result of your
actions in a situation that's unpredictable at best, and
life-threatening at worst. You step into this unknown with
an intention that comes from your core, your Essence. You
don't ask for directions; you don't ask for permission. All your
senses are activated when you step or leap into the unknown.

You sense your Essence and your purpose as a human being,
and all your knowledge, experience, skills, and abilities are at

your disposal. Courage does not limit you, whereas anxiety, cowardice, exuberance, arrogance, or recklessness will. In the state of courage, you know what's yours.

Are you willing to leave a familiar world behind?

13.2 Courageous people

Courageous people go for something because it must be done, and there is no doubt that *they* are the ones to do it. They are aware of something unseen before. They don't know if it will work, but they're willing to give it a try. There are many examples of courageous people throughout history, like Rosa Parks, Malala Yousafzai, Martin Luther King, and Mahatma Gandhi. Courageous people keep focusing on their mission and address the negative emotions that show up in their interactions with the Matrix. This makes them inspiring. They create a field to which others are attracted and in which these others are safe to think, cooperate, and co-create.

Your own everyday acts of courage may seem small in comparison to these great historical figures, but your courage is equally important because your mission will not be accomplished without it. Being courageous means that you access the strength to take risks, even if it involves facing pain or setbacks. If you act from courage, your life purpose will motivate you more than temporary safety, comfort, and satisfaction of needs and desires.

13.3 Fear and anxiety

Fear and anxiety are distinct emotions. Fear is a natural response, a biological reaction to perceived danger in the external environment. It engages the body's fight, flight, freeze, and fawn responses. This reaction is driven by the activation of the amygdala, an area in the limbic system of the brain that releases the stress hormones adrenaline and cortisol, which prepare the body for action. In moments of courage, fear remains present as the body enters a heightened state of alertness. It prepares your body and mind to confront a genuine threat. In a state of courage, this high alert can help you to move toward your goal—and act.

Courage doesn't come without fear. The American artist Georgia O'Keeffe felt the fear when she left New York and her partner Alfred Stieglitz for an adobe home in Abiquiù in the hot and lonely desert of New Mexico, with the sole purpose of finding her own painting style. Bertrand Piccard, the pilot-adventurer who was the first to fly around the world in a solar plane, answered the question of whether he experienced fear:

> *Of course, I am afraid. Anyone who does something like that without fear must be crazy. Fear is like life insurance. It increases alertness and awareness of potential problems. Fear is the red alarm.*

In contrast, anxiety is an emotion that arises when you don't feel safe due to either a potential or an undefined threat. It can originate from disturbing memories or limiting beliefs from the past. In a state of anxiety, you're overwhelmed, and you project your past into the future. You're not aware of the potential of your Essence, nor do you feel supported by others in the Matrix. You are alone.

To overcome anxiety, you need to reconnect to Essence as well as to the Matrix: Then you can access your potential, your experience, and your competence, knowing that the Matrix is there to help you make the leap into the unknown with confidence and grace. The Move On program in the next section will show you how to do this.

13.4 The language of anxiety

Anxiety manifests in the way we use language, particularly in speech patterns that avoid taking responsibility for our choices. We use words like "could," "should," "shall," "will," or "hope" that refer to the past or future, or that tend to assign power to external factors rather than to ourselves. Some examples:

- In "I could have taken the other route," the person suggests an alternative action in the past, which they didn't decide upon. However, today it's only relevant what you actually did.

- In "I should have taken that route," the person is aware of missing an opportunity and avoids responsibility for the actions they actually took.

- In "I hope things will work out," the person relies on circumstances beyond their control instead of assuming responsibility and taking appropriate action to ensure the outcome.

You may also inquire into perceived cause-and-effect relationships, using words like "because" to connect events or circumstances that are barely related: "I'm late because it rained," connects unrelated events to justify being late.

In coaching, counseling, and psychotherapy, recognizing and addressing such language patterns can be an important part of overcoming anxiety and building self-confidence.[28]

13.5 Resolving Anxiety with the Power of Words

The Logosynthesis model allows you to identify, analyze, and understand language patterns to resolve anxiety. The words you speak have the power to shape reality by directing and focusing your energy. The words you choose and the way you use them influence your thoughts, emotions, and behaviors, as well as the outcomes you create and experience in the world. By speaking specific sentences that are tailored to your situation, you can restore your energy to a flow state, thus transforming your experience and creating new avenues for your Self in the world.

The unique power of spoken words is our instrument of choice for resolving anxiety and entering a state of courage in the present moment. Once you understand the language patterns that contribute to anxiety, you can use specific sentences to shift your thoughts, emotions, and behaviors in the service of a meaningful life. You can let go of anxious thoughts and worries and live with serenity and clarity. The Logosynthesis concepts and methods have been developed in collaboration with other professionals in the field. You can find them in our books, videos, and training programs.[29]

Logosynthesis works—just say the sentences!

THE

Truth is a pathless land.
— Jiddu Krishnamurti[30]

The oldest and strongest emotion of mankind is fear,
and the oldest and strongest kind of fear is fear of the unknown.
— H.P. Lovecraft[31]

Tear up your plans.
Be wise and hold on to miracles.
They have long been recorded in the great plan.
Chase away the fears and the fear of fears.
— Mascha Kaléko[32]

You have decided to change, to leave a container, a cocoon, a safe place. Or maybe you were kicked out of it. In this empty space, your old world is gone and a new one hasn't quite arrived—yet. You lose a relationship: a parent, a partner, or a child. You leave an organization for another job or to become self-employed, or your retirement ends your role as a professional in society. You are standing on a precipice, looking into the depths, and there is nothing you can do. You meet the Void, a state of emptiness or meaninglessness in life. You feel hollow, restless, unsatisfied, depressed, anxious, angry, or irritated.

The Void tends to generate a breathtaking fear, the *horror vacui*.[33] The human mind is not made for emptiness; it has an urge to fill it with words, images, sounds, ideas, fantasies, beliefs, objects, *anything*. The Matrix in its current form is the result of generations of people filling the Void with activities that make life seem secure and predictable for us.

Strangely enough, the Void itself doesn't have any characteristics. It's neutral, not good, or bad, not positive or negative. It just is, and you're the one who gives it meaning. You can fill it with activities that create temporary relief including smoking, drinking, sex, working, games, and other forms of distraction. You can fill the Void with grief over the past or anxiety for the future. Leaving a container can be extremely challenging and you may not want to face it. You might also perceive the Void as an enormous opportunity if you've left the cage of a frozen relationship or a depressing job.

In the words of Jeremy Webb:

> *Nothing, the Void, becomes a lens through which we can explore the universe around us, and even what it is to be human. It reveals past attitudes and present thinking.*[34]

In the Logosynthesis model, the concept of the Void refers to the absence of familiar energy patterns. Though they have been useful up to now, these patterns limit your ability to tune in to the new situation. Often, they are so deeply ingrained that you notice them only when you are confronted with a completely unknown situation.

14.1 Entering the Void

When you enter the Void, it is rarely a comfortable place. Nature abhors a vacuum, and your mind does not like empty spaces either. It tends to examine reality in search of opportunities to fulfill the needs of the moment. No matter if you're hungry, thirsty, longing for activity or rest, interested, bored, or panicked, the Void won't satisfy any of these desires.

Across the centuries, people have designed many ways of avoiding confrontations with this emptiness. Because the *horror vacui* threatens security and stability in society, the Matrix designed a strategy to protect people: The awareness of the Void was suppressed, and in a strange act of magic, the horror disappeared. Strong codes against passivity and laziness were installed: Idle hands are the devil's workshop. Already by the Middle Ages, *acedia*, or sloth, was considered as one of the Seven Deadly Sins. *Sloth* was a failure to do things that one should do, indicating the vice of apathy or boredom with God.[35]

Our current culture provides continuous stimulation with the help of smartphones, tablets, and watches. People divide their waking hours between activities of work and leisure. Doing nothing is either called depression and considered an illness, or laziness, which implies selfishness and poor self-discipline.

Courage moves you away from this pattern and starts acknowledging the Void. You begin to recognize the limitations of the world you've been living in and start to notice how the Matrix restricts your choices. You notice how that feels in your mind and body. You become aware that there is a reality you don't know yet. At first, you're not cognizant of those other options. An artist stares at a blank canvas, an author sees an empty screen, and a composer listens to the sounds of nature in silence.

Embracing the emptiness that comes with not knowing takes courage. This process involves acknowledging the existence of the Void, accepting your present circumstances, and consciously letting go of unconscious patterns. This may take longer than you would prefer, as it involves resolving past issues, facing fantasies about the future, and exploring and resolving limiting beliefs. If you create a space for the Void in your life, you can expect unprocessed aspects of previous containers and roles to come to the surface of conscious awareness to be dealt with. A few examples:

■ If your relationship breaks down, you may face emotions of abandonment, rejection, fear, guilt, anger, and loss. You may need to face old beliefs about relationships that question your ability to love and to be loved in return.

■ If you are fired from a job, the Void may reveal insecurities about your talents and competence, pushing you to reassess your professional identity and future aspirations.

■ If you enter the Void after stepping back from your professional life, you might confront beliefs about productivity, purpose and value, inviting you to redefine who you are without that career.

■ If a parent dies, unprocessed emotions and unresolved experiences may arise in your grieving process, requiring you to reevaluate your relationship with your parent and in turn, your own sense of identity.

■ If you're a refugee who has left your home, culture, or country behind, facing the Void may activate feelings of unbearable homesickness and loss, while you're forced to adapt to a completely new environment.

14.2 Experiencing the Void

Confrontations with the Void come in many forms. Some are short-lived and present beneath the surface of your daily life. You may feel angry, irritable, restless, or bored, and nothing seems right. There is a strange disconnection from your normal life, physical fatigue, or a general listlessness where nothing is interesting. You're not motivated to do anything, and the meaning you used to attach to certain activities or places seems to have all but evaporated. This is normal: It's not a failure or weakness on your part, but a natural reaction to the absence of familiar landmarks and reference points. You may be aware that you're processing something deep inside that's just out of reach of your conscious mind. You may have vivid dreams. You may feel extremely sensitive or have a strong desire to hibernate.

Emotions may seem strong and raw, separated from normal context, with usual ways of coping no longer effective. You find yourself in a rich melancholy that somehow has no story at this time, unanchored and drifting, yet persistent. Be patient in these times, make space and time to meet the emptiness. Many of these reactions can be worked through using the Logosynthesis methods described in other books[36], or with the help of a professional coach, counselor, or psychotherapist. You do not have to suffer more than necessary, and you do not need to be alone.

You will also be aware of periods of profound inner stillness, emptiness, a sensory and existential vacuum without the usual distractions and noises of life. You may even find that space and time lose their linear quality and seem to dissolve. Living in the Void is being at its purest, you cannot interpret it or assign a narrative to it; it is a moment to be your Self in its most unadorned state. You cannot rush this process, nor can you sidestep it.

The Void is rarely pleasant, but there is no need to be afraid: It is part of your process of creating and moving on. In fact, you may pass through several manifestations of the Void before experiencing the profound joy of your true nature. Once you understand containers and how they work, it becomes easier to anticipate a Void, and you'll discover that it doesn't need to hurt: It just *is,* you *are*, and you can go with the flow.

14.3 Giving up roles

Experiencing the Void is not limited to those who leave a container. It can also happen if you have provided space for others and are now left behind. Children leave home, and the empty nest can be painful for the parents who made it. At the end of a school year, teachers are filled with nostalgia. When a client leaves my office after completing treatment, or when a group of trainees receives their diplomas, they may have been a part of my life for years, but now they don't need me anymore and leave an empty place in my heart.

Well-trained professionals in education and other helping professions use this empty space to reflect on the quality of their work. If they see opportunities for improvement, they may decide to undergo supervision or take advanced training to increase their efficacy with their students or clients, so that they can offer an even safer space for those who follow.

14.4 Embracing the Void

The Void may be scary, but it is also a space in which the voice and the light of your Essence can emerge. Its voice may have been muzzled, or its light has been dimmed by the rules and customs of previous containers. As you resolve the past, the Void transforms into a space filled with boundless opportunities, enabling new ideas and behaviors to develop and to take root. This ultimately leads to personal growth and transformation. To make the shift from a state of anxiety to actively moving on and shaping your reality, you need five types of courage:[37]

- The courage to learn

- The courage to practice

- The courage to act

- The courage to let go

- The courage to play

14.5 The courage to learn

To truly learn, you must be open to new ideas and willing to challenge existing beliefs. You must question, explore, and evolve these beliefs. In the Logosynthesis model, this openness is essential because it allows you to recognize and understand how outdated patterns may be shaping your life.

14.6 The courage to practice

To truly practice, you need to face and engage with the obstacles that arise when learning new skills. This involves actively shedding old habits and adopting new ones. You may try exercises to uncover hidden patterns and modify them through repetition and reinforcement. Your journey requires commitment to taking regular action and persisting, despite difficulty with change.

14.7 The courage to act

To take meaningful action, you'll need to implement the fresh insights and behaviors you've gained through your process. You must step outside your comfort zone and overcome barriers the Matrix offers you to put practice into performance. This form of courage enables you to apply what you practiced, gather feedback from those around you, integrate that feedback into new actions, and make the full transition into a new phase of your life.

14.8 The courage to let go

The courage to let go involves releasing old ways of thinking and being. This can be tedious and demanding. It may mean that you need to let go of long-held beliefs or behaviors that no longer serve you, or that you release attachments to people and situations that are not healthy or beneficial anymore. This type of courage requires you to accept the inevitability of change, and to trust that new opportunities will arise from your willingness to let go of what has been.

14.9 The courage to play

The courage to play is about more than just having fun; it's accessing your power to experiment, to make mistakes, and to explore without the burden of perfection. Playful engagement is a key component of the journey to the Void. It stimulates creativity, broadens horizons, and provides a refreshing break from rigid patterns. This form of courage allows you to view growth not just as a structured activity, but rather as a journey enriched by spontaneity and discovery. Play opens doors to new insights; it supports your path to transformation.

On your journey through the Void, you're gradually acquiring the ability to tolerate mental and emotional discomfort. You also slowly or abruptly develop a willingness to change.

By embracing the five types of courage—learning, practicing, acting, letting go, and playing—you can traverse the Void and emerge stronger, wiser, and more aligned with your Essence, as a Free Self in the Matrix, on the path of your X.

There is no specific order to the types of courage. In fact, you need all of them at any given moment. You can start by learning abstractly through literature and information from a teacher. Then, you can practice a skill and learn from experience in the safe environment of a family, a school, or a laboratory. When you begin performing in the Matrix, you may receive feedback from an unforeseen direction that compels you to venture into unfamiliar territories. And as you release your previous patterns, you need to discover new options. The same principle applies to other forms of courage.

To develop, you must be willing to learn, practice, act, let go, and play—anytime in any situation.

When we descend all the way down to the bottom of a loss, and dwell patiently with an open heart, in the darkness and pain, we can bring back up with us the sweetness of life and the exhalation of inner growth. When there is nothing left to lose, we find the true Self—the Self that is whole, the Self that is enough, the Self that no longer looks to others for definition, or completion or anything but companionship on the journey.

— Elizabeth Lesser[38]

LOGOSYNTHESIS: THE POWER
OF WORDS IN THE WORLD OF FORM

A song is sleeping in all things
It's dreaming on and on,
and the world will start to sing
once you hit the magic word
— Joseph von Eichendorff[39]

The journey through the Void is a key element of any transformation, any movement from one container, state, or role, to the next. This journey enables you to grow, to free the energy of your Self, and to align with your Essence in the Matrix you have chosen. As you embrace courage in the form of learning, practicing, acting, letting go, and play, you create a firm base for the next step in your personal evolution: Activating the power of words to shape your future reality and embody your Essence in the world of form.

In Logosynthesis, words are powerful vehicles that help you to explore and express your emotions, thoughts, values, and experiences; they also act as catalysts for change. They not only help you to describe your perceptions, emotions, and thoughts, but they also hold the potential to create, sustain, or transform your beliefs and perceptions, and the reality in which you live. In the context of this book, you can employ words to cross the Void, find a new container in the Matrix, and manifest more of your Essence in the world of form.

15.1 The Power of Words

In the Logosynthesis model, the power of words is the core mechanism for resolving blocks along your life path. If you're familiar with the model, you already know that speaking a sentence, even without any additional attention, can immediately lead to a transformation of your internal and external reality. I published an earlier version of this chapter in my book "*Discover Logosynthesis®*." If you're familiar with the model, you may want to skip these pages.

Logosynthesis starts from the basic assumption that everything that exists consists of energy organized in patterns: Solid matter with its molecules and atoms; physical energy with its frequency and field strength; and more subtle energy modes like information with bits and bytes, consciousness with thoughts and emotions, or intention based on the focused will.

Another assumption is that energy vibrates in complex patterns at different frequencies ranging from being frozen to being in flow. A third assumption states that energy either belongs to you, or it doesn't. The last of the four basic assumptions of the model contains the key working principle of Logosynthesis:

Words move energy.

When the world begins to sing, you are in contact with your deepest being, your Essence. Here the question arises: How do you find the magic word in a whole world of words?

The prevailing Western way of thinking regards words as a means of describing the world and putting it into terms—in poetry and prose, technology, and science. This is only one aspect though: Words have always been more than a tool for naming or understanding things. Words can focus the will of the speaker and thus shape reality. This is the gist of the words we use in Logosynthesis.

The real power of Logosynthesis lies in accessing and using the power of words, as it has appeared throughout the cultural and religious history of humanity. Once you accept this power, you will be able to use it as an instrument to dissolve frozen energy patterns—to remove blocks in your life. Not only that: You can activate dormant resources from your Essence and in the Matrix around you. Once you know what you need to fulfill your mission, you can use the power of words to shape reality in line with that purpose. Painful memories fade, fears disappear, and the belief in your own potential returns to you or becomes conscious for the first time. You can begin to shape reality in the service of a meaningful life.

If you're already familiar with Logosynthesis, you know that we use specific sentences to resolve limiting energy patterns. The Move On program we have designed in this book goes beyond the sentences of the Basic Procedure and removes blocks at an even deeper level.

Once you understand how Logosynthesis works and experience its elegance and effectiveness, its methods can serve as a compelling resource for fostering healing and growth, both in your personal life and in aiding others. The model helps you tap into your Essence, discover your life's purpose, and remove any obstacles on your path. Logosynthesis also integrates the potential of your body, mind, and Essence to serve your life's mission. In this process, your Free Self becomes clear and focused. While you can use Logosynthesis protocols on your own, it may be beneficial to seek support from others, especially if loneliness and abandonment have been significant themes in your life. If you are a trained professional, you can learn to use Logosynthesis to help your clients address their issues.

15.2 How does Logosynthesis work?

On the one hand, Logosynthesis supports people in returning dissociated or split-off energy to their Free Self. On the other hand, it teaches how to remove the energy of other people and objects that's stored in limiting patterns and return it to where it truly belongs.

For this purpose, it's necessary to realize that your thoughts, emotions, and beliefs as you perceive them are nothing more than energetic thought forms. Your Self creates these patterns from your energy and from the energy of other sources, reactivates them in the present, and then keeps reacting to them—over and over.

The first step in healing is to retrieve your energy that is bound in an energy pattern: a perception, a memory, a fantasy, or a belief. In a second step you return energy, related to the issue but not belonging to you, back to its origins. Finally, you retrieve your energy bound in your reactions to the pattern.

Many counseling and therapeutic methods originate from philosophy, biology, and psychology; however, they do not attribute any effects to the words themselves. Rather, language in these disciplines is used as an instrument for describing reality and for indirectly influencing the clients' worlds—by conditioning, interpretation, trance induction, anchoring, or reframing.

In contrast, Logosynthesis has specific techniques for healing and development that are based on the power of words. With the help of carefully formulated sentences, blocks on your life path are resolved. Distressing thought forms dissolve, resources are activated, and the energy previously bound up in them becomes available for you to use. This healing is profound: The release of long-stored frozen energy patterns allows your Free Self to take the stage in the Matrix.

The Logosynthesis sentences have a tangible effect. After a successful intervention, the atmosphere in the room changes, it becomes quiet in a special way: Traffic noises are muffled, and the tweeting·of birds suddenly becomes audible. Diana wrote to me shortly after treating the fear of an impending complex surgery:

> *It is now Sunday evening, and I haven't had a crying attack or any other kind of emotional collapse since yesterday afternoon. Fantastic! Every now and then I think about the fact that the surgery is imminent—and nothing dramatic happens anymore. I have the impression that the sentences are still floating and spreading in my body, establishing themselves. The process is not yet complete for my perception, but the 'drama' is almost gone—the facts gain the upper hand.*

Normally, a treated condition does not return. However, new, deeper aspects or states can emerge anytime. These are always addressed with the same procedure. The process is not always pleasant, and there are two reasons for this:

- You suddenly discover that you lack important skills or abilities. Henry discovered that he had always stayed out of conflicts or submitted to the wishes of his opponents. Once he resolved this pattern, he realized that he lacked skills to deal with conflicts. He had to attend a course to learn how to state his opinion in a convincing way. Florence didn't believe that she could finish her thesis. She was able to give up this limiting belief, but then she had to learn how to write a coherent text. In the face of new demands, old patterns of powerlessness can be reactivated. Once these are resolved, it becomes clear that the person must accept the responsibility for learning what's necessary to reach their goals in the present. The resolution usually also highlights resources that are available in the environment: Henry could attend a course and Florence could get writing advice from an experienced friend.

- Through the resolution of frozen patterns, annoying inner dialogues may disappear, but this can also lead to an inner silence that may seem oppressive or empty. In the beginning, the emptiness can seem threatening—until you start to hear the gentle, soft music of your Essence underneath.

Your life energy can be bound in many ways. The power of words releases this bound energy and makes it available to your Free Self—in the service of your mission in this life. In Part III we will describe how to make this happen. In the final part of the book, you will find examples of how to apply Logosynthesis in many different areas.

PART III

MOVE ON!

Initiating Transformation

THE ORIGIN OF
LOGOSYNTHESIS®

PART III. THE MOVE ON PROGRAM:
INITIATING TRANSFORMATION

Before one studies Zen,
mountains are mountains and waters are waters;
after a first glimpse into the truth of Zen,
mountains are no longer mountains
and waters are no longer waters;
after enlightenment,
mountains are once again mountains
and waters once again waters.

— Dōgen[40]

In out-of-the-way places of the heart,
Where your thoughts never think to wander,
This beginning has been quietly forming,
Waiting until you were ready to emerge.

For a long time it has watched your desire,
Feeling the emptiness growing inside you,
Noticing how you willed yourself on,
Still unable to leave what you had outgrown.

It watched you play with the seduction of safety
And the gray promises that sameness whispered,
Heard the waves of turmoil rise and relent,
Wondered would you always live like this.

Then the delight, when your courage kindled,
And out you stepped onto new ground,
Your eyes young again with energy and dream,
A path of plenitude opening before you.

Though your destination is not yet clear
You can trust the promise of this opening;
Unfurl yourself into the grace of beginning
That is at one with your life's desire.

Awaken your spirit to adventure;
Hold nothing back, learn to find ease in risk;
Soon you will be home in a new rhythm,
For your soul senses the world that awaits you.[41]

17

THE MOVE
ON PROGRAM

Don't prioritize your looks my friend,
as they won't last the journey.
Your sense of humor though,
will only get better with age.
Your intuition will grow
and expand like a majestic cloak of wisdom.
Your ability to choose your battles
will be fine-tuned to perfection.
Your capacity for stillness,
for living in the moment, will blossom.
Your desire to live each and every moment
will transcend all other wants.
Your instinct for knowing what (and who) is worth your time,
will grow and flourish like ivy on a castle wall.
— Donna Ashworth[42]

17.1 A path to transformation

You have now reached Part III of this book, you have
explored your purpose and the various containers in your life,
and you may be ready for *Move On*. This is a program in a
new series of Logosynthesis interventions that activate the
power of words at its deepest level.

In this section of the book, we start from the adventurous
assumption that you can reshape your reality—to align more
closely with your Free Self and your mission. The program
covers a journey from a current state, through a transformation, to a newly shaped reality that aligns with your intentions.

The program is called Move On because it uses the power of words to shape and form reality by identifying and dissolving old energy patterns and creating new ones. It follows the advanced level Logosynthesis techniques that are presented in *Alone to Alive*.

We have designed this program to help you overcome blocks and access the potential of your Essence to alter your reality in the Matrix. Move On provides a framework to either transform your current environment, or to guide your passage toward a new container, with the help of carefully designed linguistic patterns. Running the program initiates a process in which you can discover new qualities within your existing environment or discover a new direction and environment altogether.

Like every other Logosynthesis program or protocol, Move On utilizes the power of words. It contains five linguistic sequences. Each sequence contains a series of short statements that activate this power in a specific field of your Self at the intersection of your Essence and the Matrix.

17.2 The Move On program

The program starts with a *Tune In* sequence and ends with a *Tune Out* sequence. In between these, there are three other sequences: Reconnect, Release, and Restart:

Tune In ➤ Reconnect ➤ Release ➤ Restart ➤ Tune Out

Each sequence contains three to six statements which you will say several times:

Tune In

- I EXPLORE (three times)
- I ZOOM IN (twice)
- I FOCUS (once)

Reconnect

- I AM
- I KNOW
- I TRUST
- I CHOOSE
- I BELONG

Release

- I RELEASE THE PAST
- I RELEASE THE FUTURE
- I RELEASE THE MATRIX
- I RELEASE MY SELF
- I RELEASE MY ESSENCE

Restart

- I MOVE ON
- I ENTER THE NEW
- I CONNECT

- I LEARN

- I CONCEIVE

- I SHAPE

Tune Out

- Return to your issue and explore it

- Reassess your trust level

- Future pacing

- Closure

Don't be tempted to do anything with these statements just yet. Though the program may come across as simple when you first read it, the steps initiate a process that can take different lengths of time, from one hour to a few weeks or months—depending on the depth of the issues activated, your experience in working with Logosynthesis, and your level of engagement with it.

The intensity and duration aren't surprising because the Move On program accesses and resolves energy patterns at the deepest level of your being. These patterns are the building blocks of your emotions, thoughts, memories, fantasies, beliefs, values, and actions. Physical states and symptoms may come and go as part of this—because they are also energetic phenomena. The way these physical, emotional, and cognitive patterns are activated and resolved resembles what happens in deep meditation over a longer period, and the effects may be similar. Contrary to meditation though, the Move On program provides a secure framework that lays out a structure to enable you to remove blocks and disturbances considerably faster.

> *We recommend that you read the full description of the program before applying it to your own issues. Then let it sink in for a while, so that your mind can begin to understand the program in its entirety. Then go through the steps a second time to complete the exercises. If you're a professional, you must complete the program at least twice for yourself before working with clients.*

When you are ready to work, find a quiet space and at least an hour in which you won't be disturbed. Allow time for initiating each step and allowing it to work. You can interrupt or pause the protocol at any time with the help of the *Time Out* sequence. Processing time between sessions is just as important as the session itself, and a night's sleep can work wonders.

If you're experiencing a high level of stress already, we recommend that as much as possible, you reduce this distress level first, with the help of relaxation techniques you're familiar with or by using the Logosynthesis Basic Procedure found in the Appendix on page 227. Especially at the beginning, some readers may be overwhelmed by unpleasant sensations and emotions. This occurs commonly and should be expected. In time, you'll become more aware of the fact that *you are not your emotions*, even though these may feel real. If you're not used to managing intense states on your own, run the program together with a buddy or consult a trained professional to overcome possible obstacles.

Most unpleasant reactions will subside once you've become familiar with the procedure of saying the statements, letting them sink in, observing your reactions, and making a note. You may also find that you learn to perceive your reactions with curious detachment instead of owning them as parts of your identity. In later sessions, you will need less time to process single statements, and you'll reach a state of quiet balance more easily. In our own work, we often meet live with clients for the first session, which can be done either online or in our consulting rooms. In such a session, they learn how the statements work and gain confidence that intense emotions can be overcome by sticking to the clear structure of the protocol.

If you come from a therapeutic modality that emphasizes empathy and creates space for exploring and experiencing deep emotions, this program may seem counterintuitive at first. Once you realize that many emotions are just repetitive energy patterns rooted in early life events or copied from other people, you will be able to resolve them by repeating the statements of the protocol several times. This mechanism is also known as semantic satiation, though we assume that our approach works at a deeper level.[43]

17.3 The roots of the Move On program

As we discussed in our 2021 book, *Alone to Alive*, several conditions need to be met to shape reality through your Free Self:

■ An awareness of your mission in this life on planet Earth: Gaining clarity about the meaning of your life and its purpose empowers you to make decisions and take actions that align with your Essence.

- A neutral perspective of the Matrix: Developing a clear understanding of the Matrix and its functions for your Self enables you to sail through reality with awareness, grace, and ease. You start to understand the complex web of social, cultural, and personal influences that shape your experiences and beliefs, and this allows you to make conscious choices that resonate with your Free Self.

- Identifying, addressing, and resolving beliefs that limit your potential for change: By dismantling these limiting beliefs, you create a free space for growth and transformation in the context of the Matrix. You can do this by practicing the powerful techniques from *Alone to Alive*.[44]

- The experience of the Void from which the new reality can develop: Embracing the Void allows you to access and deal with the unknown and permits new pathways to emerge. In this space, you can explore new perspectives.

By recognizing, accepting, and integrating these conditions, you strengthen your connection with your Essence and empower your Free Self to tune in to the potential of the Matrix, ultimately leading to a meaningful life.

In *Alone to Alive*, we presented a protocol called The Bridge to Eternity, the first of a series of bridges in a vast archipelago. You can run this protocol to overcome any limitation you're aware of or to support you in shaping the world of form according to your mission. It consists of the following five statements:

- I AM

- I TRUST

- I KNOW

- I MOVE

- I LOVE

The Move On program expands the concepts and methods of *The Bridge to Eternity* and makes them suitable for a whole new range of applications. As in the Bridge protocol, you say a statement, let it sink in, explore your reactions, and then repeat the phrase until you reach a state of rest and relaxation. From there, you move on to the next step in the sequence or the protocol.

17.4 Logosynthesis and shaping reality—an extended perspective

In the Logosynthesis model, we assume that energy is all that exists. There is no fundamental distinction between matter and information, body and mind, or emotions and thoughts. Energy takes form through vibrations in different frequencies, with different field strengths, and in intricate patterns or fields that influence people and events. Frozen patterns can stand in the way of your healing and development. Logosynthesis methods like the Basic Procedure, Bricks, and Lego activate the power of words to dissolve these patterns.[45] [46]

In this model, matter and physical energy are associated with lower frequencies; information, consciousness, and intention vibrate at higher levels. Eventually, all energy comes from and returns to a Source that has been given many names—God, Spirit, the akashic field, the quantum field, or the zero-point field. In Logosynthesis, we use the term Essence to steer clear of connotations with other religious or spiritual systems.

Your experience of the world is heavily influenced by your beliefs, assumptions, fantasies, thoughts, values, emotions, and past experiences. They affect how you perceive, interpret, and predict events in your life, and thereby they shape your reality. For example, if someone has a deeply held belief that they are unlovable, they may interpret neutral or even positive interactions with others as evidence of this belief.

When you're aware of the potential of Logosynthesis to shift energy patterns, you can learn to identify and resolve these frozen perceptions. This opens a door through which people can begin to see and access the resources of the Matrix instead of being stuck in its limitations. Many readers of this book already know how specific words can dissolve existing energy patterns. From a Logosynthesis perspective, shaping reality is the next logical step—beyond traditional confines.

We developed the Move On program for you to design and create new energy patterns—ideas and the courage to act— in the service of your mission in this life. Different societies throughout history have constructed frameworks based on the belief that life on Earth is a source of miserable challenges to be lived through. Unlike these notions, Logosynthesis proceeds from the assumption that your life has a meaning that comes from your Essence. You can recognize this meaning and give it form, supported by resources from the Matrix.

17.5 When will you use the program?

Move On has been designed to overcome blocks to the flow of your life energy and to help you access the potential of your Essence to shape a new reality. You have already explored your existing containers with the help of the questions in part II. Move On will assist you in modifying a container or leaving it altogether, so that you can find a new one for the next stage in your development.

The Move On program influences different aspects of your Self at the interface of Essence and the Matrix—emotions, physical sensations, thoughts, values, and beliefs. The combination of the protocol and the process dissolves energy patterns that have kept you locked in limitations and restores the free flow of your life energy.

You can run the program for two types of issues, depending on your current situation:

1. Something is bothering you: You're stuck in a relationship, a job, a task, a health issue, or a financial state. You feel weary, annoyed, irritated, or blocked. Your body hurts, you feel ashamed, guilty, sad, or anxious, or you aren't making headway in your career. Often, such a state feels normal; you've been here before. *Sound familiar?*

2. You want to move on: You're aware of your mission, and you want to transform your intention into a reality in the Matrix. You are dedicated to becoming a musician, a painter, a writer, or a professional in a certain field; you want to move to another field, you want to get married, have a child, find a new job, make a career change, become self-employed, make more money, or retire. *Sound familiar?*

Usually, every issue includes components of both aspects. You may have lost contact with your Essence and therefore feel uncomfortable, or you may have lost contact with the Matrix and don't know how to recognize what you're here for.

17.6 A structured program with a protocol and a process

The overall Move On program provides a format for a transition or transformation and activates the power of words to accomplish this. This moves you into a new space for developing your Free Self. In that space, your intention from Essence creates a future that matches your mission. The Move On *program* initiates a *process* with the help of a *protocol*:

The *protocol* offers a clear structure found in the five sequences. It allows you to move on while it functions as a safety net you can fall into when you're distracted, or when intense emotions emerge. The steps of the protocol initiate a *process* that may continue long after the statements have been spoken. This process may lead you to change a limiting container, or it may function as a vehicle for you to enter and move through the Void to a new container.

The nature of the container you're entering, changing, or leaving doesn't make a difference. You leave a field that is unsafe or that limits your potential, and you enter one that expands it. The new form or the new container can be a mindset, a place, a person, a group, a team, a structure in an organization, or even another city or country. The new or modified environment will offer protection on your path and create a new, open space for your Free Self, even if you don't know what that will be at this moment.

At first sight, the steps of the Move On program might seem simpler than other methods. They do, however, require time and multiple sessions to unfold their full impact. While not a quick fix, the effects often exceed expectations. Completing the program can take from hours to weeks or even months, depending on the depth of the issue and the strength of your desire for change. Processing goes smoother and faster each time you run the protocol, especially when you leave a day or more of processing time between sessions.

Although the structure of the protocol is the same for everyone, the reactions to the statements are unique for every individual. They can vary from intense energy shifts in the body and deep sorrow, to highly spiritual insights, to everything in between. You will probably find that some sequences and statements are easier to process than others. We cannot tell you which will be the easy ones for you. This depends on the issue processed, and it has been different for every person who has tried it.

If you're relatively new to Logosynthesis, or if you're not used to addressing and processing memories, fantasies, or beliefs, we recommend practicing the Basic Procedure[47] first, as described in my book *Discover Logosynthesis*®. It can also be a good idea to run the Move On program with the help of a partner or a trained Logosynthesis Practitioner. Distressing experiences may surface, and there is no need to be alone when something unpleasant emerges.

The program will take three or more separate sessions to begin with. Allow 30 to 50 minutes for each session, but don't make it longer: Once the process is initiated, it will continue to work until the free flow of energy in your Self has been restored. This happens effectively between sessions—without any additional effort. Even after running the program, you may discover surprising new aspects for months.

If you work with a partner, it's OK to take up to an hour, but don't force anything—time is your ally. If the protocol doesn't lead to a quiet state after several repetitions of the first few statements, we recommend that you interrupt the protocol, pause for the day and start again tomorrow.

The above approach will provide the safe track you need for whatever transition you are making. As you can see from the case examples, you may need many iterations of certain statements to soften and ease a transition from darkness to the light of day. At other times, you may only say a statement two or three times before you feel your energy shift and you're smiling. Trust your intuition as you go through this program.

17.7 The protocol as a cheeseburger

The five sequences of the Move On protocol are:

1. Tune In

2. Reconnect

3. Release

4. Restart

5. Tune Out

You can easily remember the structure of the protocol if you match them with the layers of a cheeseburger:

1. *Tune In* is like the half bun that's on the bottom. Just as that half of the bun provides a solid base for the cheeseburger, Tune In sets the stage for the protocol. Everything else rests on this. It represents the initial step of exploring, zooming in, focusing, and being present for the journey ahead.

2. *Reconnect*: Lettuce adds freshness, crunch, and flavor. It is natural and green, promoting health. The Reconnect sequence emphasizes the importance of rediscovering your Free Self and connecting with Essence and with others in a healthy way.

3. *Release*: This sequence can be metaphorically represented by the beef patty in the middle of your burger. Biting into it releases the full flavor of the burger. Releasing symbolizes releasing the past and allowing new possibilities to emerge.

4. *Restart*: Can be compared to the melted cheese in your cheeseburger. Restart offers a new intensity to your process, an intensity of texture and flavor. Restart encourages you to embrace something new, learn from the wisdom of your past experiences, and restart your journey in a new way.

5. *Tune Out* represents the top part of your bun. It signifies the moment that you close your working session for now, when you disengage from the internal contents, and when you then reflect upon and integrate the experiences that were gained throughout the journey. The top bun holds everything together and in place. Tune Out provides a sense of completion and closure.

6. *Time Out* can be likened to something extra that you would add to your cheeseburger to make it the way you like it. You may decide not to add the extras, or you may add several of them. It's up to you.

BEFORE
YOU START

Running Move On requires your full presence in order to change an existing container or to move from one to the next on your life path. You can do it in your home, in a quiet and comfortable place, or outside in nature: in a park, a forest, by a river, or on the beach. The process initiated by the protocol may take longer than expected, so also allow some free time after your session. A working session can also come with surprises, and you may end up in states which need some extra attention. In this chapter you will find some suggestions to help you stay on track.

18.1 Preparation

Before you start, download, print, and prepare the Quick Reference sheet to have the steps of the protocol in front of you.[48] Then set up your laptop, tablet, or drawing and writing materials. Have a glass of water ready and find possible issues. Then Tune In!

18.2 Suggested session length and content

We recommend that you plan enough time for the program. A full cycle of Move On can easily last days, weeks, or even months. Count with at least three sessions of about an hour on consecutive days to completely resolve an issue. To begin with, we suggest that you plan these three sessions, starting with *Tune In and Reconnect*, adding *Release and Restart* in the second and third session.

Session 1: Tune In, Reconnect, Tune Out

Session 2: Tune In, Reconnect, Release, Tune Out

Session 3: Tune In, Reconnect, Release, Restart, Tune Out

This is a *suggested* structure. You may be able to process more, or you may only process one or two statements in a session. There are no hard and fast rules regarding how much you do. There are no *shoulds*. It depends on the issue you're working on and what becomes activated for you. Go slowly and take care. As you become familiar with this way of working, you will be intuitively guided, and you'll know what is right for you at any given time.

18.3 Repeat statements sooner rather than later

As you speak and repeat statements, some of them will lead to a state of relaxation quickly and easily. You won't need many iterations, and you may not feel intense reactions. Other statements will be less easy to process: There is energy bound in them, and they will take many repetitions. This occurs regularly. It is extremely important to remember that *you do not need to suffer*. There is no necessity to become overwhelmed and end up feeling worse than you did before you started the program. You can avoid this by repeating the statement at the first sign of discomfort or distress. If that doesn't reduce the distress level, run a Time Out as described below in Chapter 24. This will ensure that your energy stays in continuous motion, and you will not unnecessarily flooded by emotion.

18.4 Making notes

Making notes helps you to stay grounded. You say a statement, let it sink in and work, then briefly return to your adult awareness in the present to make a note of what happened. This can seem awkward at first, and it is different from other Logosynthesis protocols, but you will quickly get into a rhythm of saying a statement, letting it sink in, making a note, and returning to the protocol. This structure is stabilizing in itself.

Making notes also allows you to remember your experience during the process and offers an opportunity to integrate the emerged material later. Once frozen patterns have been dissolved, it can be difficult to even remember them.

Keep your notes short. Write down what you observed:

■ Emotions: joyful, sad, anxious, disgusted, angry, surprised, ashamed, guilty, curious…

■ Thoughts, opinions, and judgments about yourself, others, and the world

■ Physical sensations: rapid heartbeat, sweating or coldness, tightness in your chest, a headache, a dry mouth, fatigue, muscle tension, drowsiness, or dizziness

■ Memories: scenes from the past and your reactions to them

■ Fantasies: what could, should, or might happen

■ Avoidance patterns: a tendency to open your mailbox, read the news, play computer games, take a nap, make a shopping list, or wonder what you will make for dinner…

Writing down all these reactions breaks the archaic connection between a statement and your reactions to it. This will reduce your distress level and help to support the resolution of whatever is activated in the process. Remember: You are not your reactions—you experience them, and they can and will change over time.

18.5 About the exercises in this part of the book

In this and the following chapters, we'll explain each of the statements in the five sequences of the Move On protocol. We'll also offer a short exercise: You say a statement, you explore your reactions to it, you make a note, and you repeat that procedure two more times.

These exercises help you to explore and get used to the technique and to the effects of a statement without getting too involved in reactions. If you go with the flow, you'll discover that the statements can generate a wide array of reactions. Just observe these reactions: There is no need to further explore or do anything else at this moment.

18.6 Saying the statements

The way you work with each of the statements in the Move On program is always the same, no matter what the statement is or how you react to it:

▪ You say the statement out loud

▪ Let it sink in

▪ Make a short note of your physical, emotional, and mental reactions

18.7 Additional pointers

▪ Each working session begins with the Tune In sequence and ends with the Tune Out sequence. Between Tune In and Tune Out you complete as much or as little as you can comfortably manage. On some days that will be a single statement, on others it may be two full sequences of statements or even the whole program.

▪ You are activating unconscious patterns throughout your system. It's not necessary to be aware of these aspects at a conscious level; it's enough to initiate the process with the statements, observe what's happening, make notes, and let the power of words do the work.

▪ You may switch to Time Out and then Tune Out anytime: If your time is up, if you're tired, or if it's just too intense. If you tune in again the next day, you will notice that the process has continued under the surface of your normal daily consciousness.

▪ We recommend starting with Tune In and ending with Tune Out every time you use the protocol, regardless of how much has been processed in between.

▪ Most people who tested the program were able to access more resources with every additional cycle of the protocol— or parts of it. They resolved more frozen patterns, and the amount of their free energy increased.

▪ It's quite common to work with only two or three statements in a session. The good news is that if a statement or a sequence has taken a long time to work through at the beginning, it will be much faster in subsequent sessions—even if you address an entirely different issue.

■ If you're stuck after several iterations of a statement, you can interrupt processing with a *Time Out*. After that, you can *Tune Out* or neutralize reaction patterns—with the help of the Logosynthesis Basic Procedure or with other techniques, you're familiar with. This can also be helpful if a memory, fantasy, or belief becomes active.

■ We print all statements of the protocol in capitals to emphasize their potential to invoke the power of words.

The Move On protocol starts with *Tune In*. This sequence sets the stage for all the processing you will do. In our cheeseburger metaphor, Tune In is the half bun at the bottom. Everything else rests on it. It represents the initial step of exploring, zooming in, focusing, and being present for the journey ahead. Just as the two halves of the hamburger bun hold everything together, Tune In and Tune Out do the same for you.

The Tune In sequence consists of the following steps:

- Choosing an issue

- Assessing your trust level

- Exploring the issue

- Zooming in to deeper levels of the issue

- Focusing the issue at the deepest level

- Finding a symbol (image, perception, word or metaphor)

The rest of this chapter contains a description of these steps.

19.1 Choosing an issue

The Tune In sequence of the Move On protocol helps you to identify and engage with existing energy patterns—the conditions or circumstances you wish to alter. After identifying an issue you're using the power of words to explore, zoom in, and focus on deeper levels within that *issue*. In this context, I prefer the word issue: The word *problem* suggests that there is a solution, and the effects of the Move On program can go far beyond single solutions for single problems.

When people try to solve a problem, they often try to figure out what's wrong and put it into words. They then look for reasons why it went wrong, explore options, decide what to do, and then act on that decision. This approach works for many everyday themes, especially when the problem is clear, and solutions are available. You're hungry, so you get something to eat; you're tired, so you rest; you're bored, so you call a friend. When the lights go out, you check the fuses. Solutions are logical and rational: If something is wrong, you can do something about it. Following a strategy that reduces issues to solvable problems is often successful. Sometimes, however, a situation has so many aspects that your rational mind is overwhelmed with explanations and options, and your intuition is misdirected or even muted. When you get stuck like this, it's time to Move On.

In the Move On program, identifying an issue is the first step of a longer exploration using the Tune In sequence. On the surface, an issue or a symptom may seem clear, but when it comes to changing something, the subject may suddenly become elusive. Even when you're aware of your mission, the Matrix can send confusing messages which sometimes support it while at other times the people and circumstances in the Matrix seem to sabotage your well-meaning intentions.

The Tune In sequence helps you to access and explore aspects that may be hidden under the surface of the issue you identified. It moves you away from a rational style of problem-solving to a deeper assessment that involves every aspect of your being—your Essence, your Self, and the Matrix. Then, everything you've ever learned and experienced becomes available for you to use.

19.2 Identify an issue

Now take some time to do an inquiry into your current state or circumstances and explore what you want to happen and what's standing in the way. Answer the following questions and make some notes:

■ *How do you name the state or situation you want to change?*

■ *What do you experience, feel, or sense in your body?*

■ *Which emotions show up in this process?*

■ *Which thoughts, values, memories, fantasies, and beliefs come to the foreground?*

■ *Which behavior patterns are attached to this state?*

Your answers to these questions are the starting point for further exploration using the Tune In sequence.

19.3 Assess your trust level

After you have selected an issue and answered the above questions, the Tune In sequence begins with an assessment of your trust level. This is useful to track your progress and development over time. When you compare your trust level before and after the protocol steps, you can see how far you've come. If your trust level is high, it may indicate that your goals are within reach; if it's low, there's more work to do in exploring and resolving frozen patterns. Assessing your trust level will make you more aware of your strengths and weaknesses and will guide your focus for continued use of the Move On program.

Assess your trust level related to the issue you found—on a scale from 1 to 10. A 1 means you have minimal trust; you don't have a clue how you will ever get from A to B. A score of 10 means you fully trust your skills, knowledge, and experience, and you know where to go and what to do. Typically, your trust level will be lower at the beginning of a session and higher at the end.

19.4 Explore, zoom in, and focus

Most of your emotions, thoughts, and actions in any given moment are neither rational nor fully conscious. They are an automatic continuation of ideas and actions that were installed early on in your life. On your path to adulthood, some of those patterns became more stable, while others were erased. Your mind created a frame of reference with elements from the families of your mother and father, which in turn were embedded in the Matrix of life on the planet during a certain time. You learned what you should do and shouldn't, and what you can and can't do.

People are often unaware of the roots of an issue. They tend to attribute problems to misfortune, to mistakes they've made, or to other people and circumstances in their current environment. They don't realize that they keep repeating the same templates in relationships and work situations, and that these patterns show a striking similarity with what happened to them at school or at home when they were children.

In contrast to conventional problem-solving approaches, the Move On program is not based on logic. You don't need to know *why* you have this issue, *where* it came from, or *how* to cope with it. If you run the program, you'll know more in the end, in ways you couldn't have imagined before.

After finding an issue, answering the questions, and assessing your trust level, you unveil a deeper level of the issue identified by activating the power of words in the statements of the Tune In sequence: I EXPLORE, I ZOOM IN, and I FOCUS.

19.5 I EXPLORE

The statement I EXPLORE initiates a search for the deepest cause of the issue that has shown up at the surface. You say this *three times*. The outcome of this search is neither logical nor predictable. If a client in my consulting room describes a problem they experience in their daily life, and I invite them to say the statement I EXPLORE and to let it sink in, they encounter a vast array of images, metaphors, memories, fantasies, and beliefs they wouldn't have imagined in their wildest dreams. You say I EXPLORE *three* times and let it sink in.

19.6 I ZOOM IN

Saying and processing I EXPLORE allows you to dive under the surface of the issue and discover deeper levels. The next step invites your subconscious mind to become more specific by means of the statement I ZOOM IN. You say this statement *twice* and let it sink in, making a note each time. When people say and repeat the Zoom statement, they sometimes notice logical steps. At other times, their reactions are completely associative, or they perceive nothing at all. You don't need to think about what comes up when you say this or any of the statements: You go with the flow, let it sink in while you observe your reactions, make your notes, and you continue in that rhythm, regardless of what shows up.

19.7 I FOCUS

After exploring and zooming in, you now let your subconscious mind find a form or an aspect of the issue to be processed today by saying I FOCUS. You do this *once*. The result from this step offers the content for the Move On protocol. We'll describe possible forms of this content below.

19.8 Find a symbol

After exploring, zooming in, and focusing, a word, image, thought, perception, or metaphor often emerges. You may also notice a memory, or a fantasy. Sometimes there is what seems to be nothing: a cloud, a haze, a fog, or a color. That's also fine: It does not need to make sense. Whatever shows up represents the theme for the remainder of the protocol. Write down the word you found or draw the symbol on a sheet of paper, and you're ready for the Reconnect sequence.

19.9 Raya Tunes In

How do you name the state or situation you want to change?

Starting issue: I want to increase my physical fitness.

What do you experience, feel, or sense in your body?

Heaviness in my body, weight on my shoulders

Which emotions show up in this process?

Sadness, depression, weariness

Which thoughts, values, memories, fantasies, and beliefs come to the foreground?

Getting fit and healthy is such a long road…it will be difficult…I won't like it; it will be an effort. The thought of the effort makes me feel tired already!

Which behavior patterns are attached to this state?

Patterns of how I move, live, sleep etc. that have become habits in recent years.

Trust level that this can be resolved: 3.

I EXPLORE

- *Would I really be able to do it?*

- *I'm thinking about all the activity that happens in the gym*

- *I see an image of my feet in my walking shoes*

I ZOOM IN

- *I see my feet walking on a treadmill*

- *I notice the rhythm of the movement*

I FOCUS

- *I realize that I don't know if I want to walk or go to the gym, there's conflict.*

Metaphor or symbol: *An image of how I walk when I'm tired.*

19.10 Practice Tune In

- Pick an issue and reflect on it with the help of the questions above.

- Assess your trust level 1-10. How confident are you that this issue can be resolved at this time?

- Say I EXPLORE, three times. Let the words sink in each time. Observe your reactions in your body, your thoughts, and your emotions. Make a note.

- Say I ZOOM IN twice. Let the words sink in each time. Observe your reactions, and make a note.

- Say I FOCUS once. Let the words sink in. Observe your reactions, and make a note.

- Create a symbol: What word, thought, image, perception or a metaphor represents your focus?

- Make a note or drawing of this symbol.

Now you're ready to Reconnect. But first a few words about Tuning Out...

20

TUNE
OUT

*After a while, you learn to ignore
the names people call you
and just trust who you are.*
— Shrek the Third[49]

In the same way you Tune In to the Move On protocol from your everyday life, you Tune Out when you leave it. The Tune Out sequence is represented by the top of the cheeseburger bun. It protects space for all the other ingredients, allowing them to be contained, combined, and complete. In Tune Out, you explore and reflect on the changes that have occurred during the application of the protocol. You also reassess your trust level and your inner state regarding your initial issue. This chapter describes the sequence we developed for this purpose. We're putting it here to emphasize that it's OK to go into this sequence at any point in time.

20.1 When do you go to Tune Out?

You can run the Tune Out sequence after tuning in and having worked through one, two, or three sequences, or after just a single statement. It doesn't matter how far you get. Most people can comfortably manage one to five statements of the Reconnect sequence in their first session, then they add some or all the statements of the Release sequence in the second session, and run Reconnect, Release, and Restart in a session after that. *Do not use all sequences in the first session.*

You can interrupt the Move On protocol to Tune Out at any point: The statement(s) that you've worked with will continue to work within your system between sessions, and what's too heavy or intense during the day may soften or settle during the night.

There are various reasons for tuning out:

- You have gone through all the statements of one or more sequences: Reconnect in the first session, Reconnect and Release in the second session, or Reconnect, Release, and Restart in the third session.

- The time available in a session of 30-50 minutes is too short to run a full sequence or the whole protocol, especially in the first sessions.

- Nothing seems to happen, even after many iterations of single statements. This means it may be too early to go deeper or any farther at this moment. Remember that you created these patterns at an early moment in your life, and you may not yet be ready to give them up.

- You feel drowsy, tired, or even exhausted when you're resolving frozen patterns. This happens because many layers and patterns have been stirred up in your energy system. This is normal in the Move On process and perfectly OK. When you react like this, drink one or more glasses of water first. Usually this helps with restoring your energy flow. If it doesn't, take a Time Out, then move to Tune Out.

- You also move to the Tune Out sequence if intense emotions come up that don't disappear with seven or more iterations. Write down your experiences, drink water, eat something, or take a walk. You may also want to share what happened with a friend, partner, or family member.

20.2 The Tune Out sequence

The Tune Out sequence guides you through steps of reflection and closure. Each step has a specific purpose and is designed to support your whole system. Let's look at each step in more detail:

1. Remember your symbol, your focus: Return to the symbol, image, or word you found as a representation for your focus. Examine what has happened to this symbol.

2. Return to the issue you started with and explore your reactions to this issue now. Reevaluate the issue from the perspective of any new insights that you have gained.

3. Reassess your trust level on the scale of 1-10. How is it different, and what is different?

4. Future pacing: Envision how things will be different moving forward. Imagine outcomes and anticipate the impact of your growth and transformation on future experiences. Identify possible next issues and write them down for a future session.

5. Leave the room or the environment where you ran the protocol and don't reflect on it any further. Everything happened that could happen, and the process will continue without any conscious intervention.

6. Drink water, rest and relax.

The steps of the Tune Out sequence provide a frame to reflect, reassess, and conclude the protocol. They will promote a sense of closure and integration regarding any insights you have gained. Tune Out also identifies unresolved aspects to pick up on next time.

20.3 Christopher Tunes Out

I feel like I've been somewhere! Wow! I'm quite tired now… I made the metaphor of a door key, which represented how I would unlock the door to the future that I really want. My trust level was a 3. Now, when I go to find the key, I see it as part of the keyring I use all the time. Before, it was a single key in my hand, separate from the others. It's become part of my normal life now, something I use/do and not just a dream. My trust level is 8 now. I feel really good! Like it's possible, that it could be real. My reactions, I felt energy shifting around my body and I remembered several interactions with team members over the last few months, I saw faces, heard the words again…I see that I have been getting more and more restless. I realize that I don't need to listen to everyone, listening was an important and 'good' behavior in my home when I was growing up and sometimes, I think I do it more than is necessary… I'll think about that some more… For the future, I can take the research that I've done re starting my business seriously now, it's not just something I'm playing with. I know what I need to do!

20.4 Practice Tune Out

■ Go back to the symbol you created for your focus.

■ Explore how it changed, and what it means for you.

■ Return to the issue you started with and observe your reactions to it now. Reevaluate the issue in the light of any new insights you have gained.

■ Reassess your trust level. Has it changed? If so, how do you experience this difference?

■ Imagine your future Self regarding this issue. What will be different? How are your thinking, emotions, and behavior affected? What will you do that you haven't done before?

■ What issues arose you need to work on in the future?

■ Leave your current environment and do something else now.

THE RECONNECT
SEQUENCE

You protect yourself from blockage
by becoming transparent to the transcendent.
— Karlfried Graf Dürckheim[50]

21.1 Meeting the Matrix from Essence

Your Self on this planet is an interesting phenomenon. It emerges as a manifestation of Essence in its eternal expansion. Essence has provided you with a body, a mind, and a task for this life which may include to experience, to learn, to explore, to support, to teach, to play, to perform, or to just be. That same Self is also a citizen of the Matrix, with its vast collection of socio-energetic fields and their associated rules, codes, laws, limits, and resources.

In my previous Logosynthesis books, I put a lot of emphasis on reconnecting to your Essence: It's the source of your life energy and gives meaning to your life on the planet. In more recent years we have discovered that it's just as important to stay connected to the Matrix: It's what allows you to love and live with other people, and it offers access to resources that are needed for your mission.

Access from your Free Self to your Essence and to the Matrix is vital to your existence. An obstructed flow of life energy can lead to various obstacles:

▪ You're aware of your mission in life, but you seem to be the only one. Nobody seems to resonate with you, and you experience the Matrix as a cold, aloof environment that keeps you at a distance or even actively rejects you.

- You have access to the resources provided by the Matrix, but you're not happy or satisfied. Your mental and material needs, wishes, and desires are fulfilled, and there is no reason to complain about anything. However, deep in your heart, something is missing: your connection to who and what you really are—Essence.

- You're stuck in between: The world doesn't seem to offer what you want or need. Your relationships aren't satisfying, you don't have a job, or your job doesn't appeal to you anymore. Your health isn't good, and there's too much month left at the end of your money. Life doesn't make sense: You're disconnected from the Matrix as well as your Essence.

21.2 The Reconnect sequence of the Move On protocol

The Reconnect sequence is the aspect of Move On that gets your energy flowing again, repairing any weakness or damage to your connections to Essence or the Matrix. Reconnect is represented by the healthy, crisp, green lettuce in the cheeseburger image.

We often find that the individual statements in this sequence take the longest to process. Most people's belief systems are alienated or disconnected from the inherent meaning of these five statements. They immediately associate them with diminishing nouns or adjectives, like "I AM wrong," "I AM stupid," "I AM worth nothing." To I KNOW, people add "nothing," and they complete the I TRUST statement with "no one." How can we restore the original meaning of these statements, the fact that it's your birthright to be, to know, to trust, to choose how to live your life, and to belong?

The Move On program is designed to do just that, acknowledging that some people are a million miles away from the awareness of their divine origin, their mission in the world, and their ability to use resources from the Matrix. It's heartbreaking for me to see, over and over again, how a disconnection from Essence—and the projection of this disconnection into the Matrix—leads to deep misery and unhappiness.

In working with the program ourselves, we have learned that it is possible to regain access to the resources of Essence as well as to the Matrix once we melt the ice. This ice has often been frozen for generations, in families that never learned to allow love and affection to surface—out of a fear of being hurt even more deeply.

It's the purpose of the Reconnect sequence to connect your Self to your Essence and to the Matrix you have chosen. You will better recognize your mission and the resources of the Matrix while in such a connected state. The sequence restores the free flow of energy in your Self, with the help of five short statements:

- I AM

- I KNOW

- I TRUST

- I CHOOSE

- I BELONG

21.3 The effect of the statements

The statements of the Move On protocol are designed to unlock the energy necessary to shape your future. Each statement in the sequences starts with the word "I," followed by an action verb. From the perspective of Logosynthesis, these statements receive their strength from your Essence. Every time you use the word "I" in a statement, the power of words activates your Free Self at the intersection of your Essence and the Matrix. As a result, a specific aspect of your reality in the Matrix is reshaped in a new and distinct way.

Each statement of the Reconnect sequence represents an aspect of your Free Self in the world. You say each statement out loud several times and let it sink in, just as you did in the Tune In sequence. Each time you do this, you move into a mental state from which you can observe what happens in response to it. The content of the words you speak kindles an intention to create a new reality based on that content. Any reaction to a statement represents the part of your frame of reference that still clings to old reference points. It is easy to get distracted by the needs of your body and mind, and you may need to repeat each statement many times to stay on track.

21.4 Exploring Reactions

When you observe your reactions, you'll see that they come from familiar sources: The emerging thoughts and emotions are recurring patterns in your frame of reference. In our trials, many participants reacted in ways that contradicted the statement they heard. Responses ranged from doubts like "That can't be true," to strong emotions such as grief, anger, or fear.

Others felt physical discomfort, such as tension in the neck, or recalled painful memories. Often, people would initially respond from a rigid mindset. For example, statements like I AM, I KNOW, or I TRUST were often completed with limiting beliefs:

- *I AM ... vulnerable*

- *I KNOW ... nothing*

- *I TRUST ... nobody*

Other reactions triggered physical, emotional, or mental symptoms like:

- *My legs feel heavy like lead*

- *Internal conflict between letting go and holding on*

- *My baby self is sobbing*

- *My mind is blank*

- *I'm scared...*

- *Tears in my eyes*

- *I'm so angry!*

Such reactions come from frozen patterns in one's energy system. However, it's fascinating to see how these reactions shift. Changes occur when you repeat a statement, observe your reactions, and take notes. Over time, repeating the statement erases old response patterns. The repetitions lead to a state where old reactions are no longer triggered. This new state is often described as relaxed, quiet, strong, curious, or open. The repetition does the work, making the statement eventually true. Once our participants recognized the deeper truth in a statement, they were able to fully embrace it. They described their state after saying a statement and letting it sink in, in a variety of ways:

- *My body relaxes, and my head screams that this is nonsense!*

- *It was just a dream*

- *I feel an enormous energy shift*

- *I'm very strong all the way from head to toe*

- *I'm present now*

- *It feels like integration*

- *A lot stronger in my body, especially in my head*

- *This feels good!*

and the most important one:

- *YES!*

You'll discover that being in itself is free from restrictions. The statement "I AM" will resonate with you, boosting your confidence. No one can take away your being, but it may require time and repetition to grasp this at its deepest level. If discomfort persists after 20-30 repetitions, take a break, move to Time Out and Tune Out, and try again tomorrow.

Thoroughly process a statement before moving on to the next one. Each new statement addresses and clears more fixed patterns in your energy system. As a result, your thoughts, emotions, and sensations shift, leading you towards greater autonomy. It's surprising for many that such brief statements can be so impactful. Some tend to rush to the next statement quickly. However, taking the time to reflect on each repetition yields deeper insights and a more significant effect. When a statement brings relaxation and peace, you're ready to move on to the next one.

Now we'll take a closer look at each statement of the Reconnect sequence.

21.5 I AM

The Reconnect sequence starts with I AM. This statement expresses the fact that you are a being beyond space and time, on a journey of eternal exploration and development. In this life, your Essence has set an intention and created a seed for it in the Matrix. That seed, your Self, is planted in an environment to become what it's been designed for. Saying I AM makes it clear that this Self exists in space and time.

Saying and repeating I AM lifts the veil that the Matrix has pulled over your eyes. You don't need to prove who you are, or that you are—to anyone. You don't need to justify your existence to others who may want you to adopt their ideas or adapt to their opinions. The power of words in I AM puts your existence into the only real perspective: You are Essence, a being beyond space and time. Saying I AM confirms that your Essence has chosen to be your Self are at this time in history: You are here, now.

Once the statement I AM becomes true, you arrive in this world. You're in contact with Essence, and you're in contact with the Matrix. You are aware of your mission and the potential that comes with it. You can activate the resources of

the Matrix necessary for that mission. If you can say I AM
from the bottom of your heart, you don't need any additional
sentences: It's the most powerful mantra you can imagine.
However, you don't need to reach for the sky without a ladder,
and that's why the Reconnect sequence contains other statements that each cover a certain aspect of living on this planet.

 I AM doesn't always come easy. On the contrary: Some of
the statements easily require up to 30 or 40 iterations. These
repetitions can take a long time and can be challenging, even
disturbing, if you identify with your reactions instead of
observing them from a healthy distance. When you're nearing your resource state, you'll notice that your speaker and
observer in your Self become one—in a new, lively way.

21.6 Lily's reactions to I AM

Lily, our artist from previous chapters, needed 16 iterations to
reach a resource state in reaction to I AM:

1. I know that I am smart, resourceful, and talented, and yet…

2. Sadness, being burdened

3. A heavy feeling in my chest, like a weight

4. A little calmer, the heavy weight is still there

*5. Sigh. I just have to white knuckle through it, it's burning up a
lot of energy*

6. I feel calmer, a little bit of that weight is still there

7. Pressure is moving a little bit lower, heavy on my chest again

8. Better, sense of calm, the heaviness is less

9. Image of the cobwebs came back and just receded

10. Image of one wall section that I keep on washing

11. Tingling in my upper chest, energy moving, resolving

12. Image of sand moving downward in a funnel, an hourglass

13. Mental picture of a form moving away from me in space

14. Relaxation

15. A tingling in my upper chest

16. Calm

From here she moved to I KNOW.

21.7 Practice I AM

Do this exercise without Tuning In, you don't need to focus on an issue. Say the statement I AM. Let it sink in for a moment and pay attention to your reactions—in your body, your thoughts, and your emotions. Write down these reactions, even if they seem silly or strange. Do this three times. This will allow you to become familiar with how you react to the statement without the added intensity of a painful issue. Then put your notes in a file. You can review them later and use them for future sessions.

21.8 I KNOW

The statement I KNOW brings the core of your being to the surface of your consciousness. If you know, you recognize truth in every moment of your life, and you're neither distracted by the noise and haste flooding in from the Matrix, nor are you overwhelmed by the continuous flow of signals from your body and mind: Physical sensations, needs, emotions, wishes, reflexes, intrusive thoughts, and all kinds of other patterns. This kind of knowing is what is meant in the Desiderata, by Max Ehrmann:[51]

> *Go placidly amid the noise and the haste*
> *and remember what peace there may be in silence.*

I KNOW without any attachments represents the deepest form of knowledge in the Universe: You know you are connected; You are evidence of a higher consciousness in a temporal human body. You know, and this form of knowing is unshakeable.

If you add something to I KNOW—facts, fields, skills, techniques, or experience—this knowledge will always be partial, limited. I KNOW may then sound pretentious or arrogant. In the Matrix, there's always more to know. If something like an ultimate truth exists, I KNOW will bring you closer to it. The Matrix will always distract you from that truth, as illustrated in the following story, told by Jiddu Krishnamurti:[52]

> *You may remember the story of how the devil and a*
> *friend of his were walking down the street, when they*
> *saw ahead of them a man stoop down and pick up*
> *something from the ground, look at it, and put it away*
> *in his pocket. The friend said to the devil, "What did*
> *that man pick up?" "He picked up a piece of Truth,"*
> *said the devil. "That is a very bad business for you,*
> *then," said his friend. "Oh, not at all,"the devil replied,*
> *"I am going to let him organize it."*

21.9 Lily's reactions to I KNOW

To fully integrate the I KNOW statement, Lily needed 23
iterations:

*1. A mental picture of space in my head, right below my brow,
interesting, smiling*

*2. Same sensations moving toward the back in my brain…
A lot going on there*

3. Similar, moving down the back of my brain stem

4. Know how to be successful

5. (crying) *For the past two weeks I have lost my connection with
what feeds my soul… Don't know how to bring into alignment*

6. I'll figure it out, I always do

*7. Pressure in esophagus like I swallowed something. What a
metaphor is that!*

8. I am crying, that's my reaction

9. I cry when I need to release energy, and that's my way

10. Feeling a surge of electricity through my body, tingling

*11. Like: Who am I kidding? I can't do this! I have too much
imprint from childhood!*

12. My cousins I never perceived as supporting me, but they did.

13. Thinking about a helpful text message this morning

*14. Thinking about what I told you… All complicated stories
which are tangled*

*15. Calmer and simultaneously a form is moving away in space…
Something is moving down my esophagus*

*16. Calmer and again the mental picture that something is going
down my esophagus*

17. Calmer but it's stuck

18. Moving down my esophagus

*19. There is new lump I swallowed, and it's slowly going down
and meeting the first one*

20. My neck and my shoulders, carrying the weight of the world

*21. Sensing the introject of my grandmother's body, raising seven
children. She was forced to do that. I'm somehow carrying on that
tradition, and that's not what I want*

22. The image of the spider webs came back and went away

23. Calm now

We stopped here because Lily was in a quiet state, and we
were near the end of the hour. We went to the Tune Out
sequence, and I asked Lily to return to the symbol she started
with. It was gone. When I asked her to return to the issue she
had presented, she said:

> *I'm going to put one foot in front of the other, doing the
> best I can. Still feel a hopelessness and futility, to make
> the plane fly. I've been doing this a long time. Right at
> this moment I feel I'm able to compartmentalize it in
> the service of what I'm here to do.*

In this first session, Lily's trust level had risen from a 2 to a 6, just by speaking the statements I AM, and I KNOW, and letting those words do the work.

21.10 Practice I KNOW

Do this exercise without Tuning In, you don't need to focus on an issue. Say the statement I KNOW. Let it sink in for a moment and pay attention to your reactions—in your body, your thoughts, and your emotions. Write down these reactions, even if they seem silly or strange. Do this three times. You will become familiar with how you react to the statement without the added intensity of a painful issue. Then put your notes in a file. You can review them later and use them for future sessions.

21.11 I TRUST

The statement I TRUST contains the basic assumption that you're not alone in this universe. If I AM and I KNOW are true for you, there will be a deep understanding that you're safe, connected to Essence, and you bring this connection into the world with your mission. If you trust, you also know that there will be resources in the Matrix, even if you haven't found them—yet.

If you associate your security with the Matrix—depending on people, status, an identity, a profession, health, or wealth—the deeper truth in I TRUST will seem fuzzy. It's great to trust your partner, your family, your body, your finances, your expertise, or your experience, but all these pillars of security may crumble in uncertain times. On the other hand, if you only trust Essence, God, or Allah, you may also get into trouble, as depicted in the following story:[53]

> *A man was trapped on his roof-top during a flood.*
> *First, his neighbor passed by in a rubber dinghy and*
> *asked him to jump in. "No thank you," he said, "God*
> *will provide." He gave the same reply when a police*
> *speedboat and then a military helicopter offered to res-*
> *cue him. When he died and went to heaven, he blamed*
> *God of not saving him. God kindly said: "I sent you*
> *two boats and a helicopter, what else did you expect?"*

Another variation of this theme is attributed to the prophet
Muhammad:[54]

> *When Muhammad saw a Bedouin leaving his camel*
> *without tying it, he asked him why he was doing this.*
> *The Bedouin replied that he trusted in Allah and had*
> *no need to tie the camel. The Prophet replied, "Trust in*
> *Allah, but tie your camel!"*

The pandemic, the ongoing wars, and the rapidly changing
climate have shown that much of what we have previously
relied upon in the Matrix is brittle. The events of the past few
years have shown that the healthcare system, the political order based on international treaties, and the way we have used
nature's resources in the service of our economy are more
fragile than we would have ever expected.

If you are, and if you know, you will develop a deep state of
trust—in Essence as well as in the Matrix. You are aware of
your potential and you're able to activate it at any moment
through your Free Self. In trust, you experientially know that
the core of your being is indestructible, as beautifully stated
by Franz Kafka:[55]

In theory, there is a possibility of perfect happiness: To believe in the indestructible element within one, and not to strive towards it.

I TRUST is also a state of being and knowing—at root level they go together and represent perfect happiness in unity. Kafka was aware of how difficult it is to access this state and probably used the words "in theory" on purpose.

21.12 Lily's reactions to I TRUST

In her second session, Lily started the protocol from the beginning. This time, I AM and I KNOW easily led to curiosity and joy, but I TRUST needed 31 iterations:

1. Dissociated

2. Funny feeling in stomach … uneasiness

3. Slight nausea

4. More nauseous

5. Less nausea

6. Air in my throat

7. Cold air in my mouth

8. Cold air going up into my nasal passages

9. Cold air moving up, head pounding a little

10. Statement feels untrue for me

11. No, I don't

12. That doesn't feel true

13. Disconnected

14. Impatient

15. Calmer

16. It feels scary.

17. Said it loudly; trying to convince myself

18. Questioning tone of (inner) voice

19. An exhortation that I don't really believe

20. OK but disconnected

21. Disconnected

22. Warm dry feeling in throat

23. OK

24. Not sure if I can trust

25. Feels neutral

26. Neutral

27. Cool air in throat

28. Took a cleansing breath

29. Neutral

30. A calm happy sensation; excitement

31. Something has shifted. I feel a sense of excitement!

21.13 Practice I TRUST

Say the statement I TRUST. Let it sink in for a moment and pay attention to your reactions—in your body, your thoughts, and your emotions. Write down these reactions, even if they seem silly or strange. Do this three times. You will become familiar with how you react to the statement without the added intensity of a painful issue. Then put your notes in a file.

21.14 I CHOOSE

Choices are everywhere, all the time, from daily decisions about what to wear or what to eat, to lifetime decisions about a partner, a career, or a home.

If you are, you know, and you trust, then you have access to an infinite realm of options—both in Essence and in the Matrix: You've got the power to choose. You connect your Essence to a decision in the context of the Matrix. You know what's important, and you trust your judgment. You are familiar with the strong and weak characteristics of your body and mind, you can distinguish friends from foes, and—crucially—you know what you're here for. This perspective enables you to make decisions.

How have you chosen a partner, a profession, a job, or a place to live? If you're satisfied with these decisions, they may be based on a combination of guidance from your Essence on the one hand, and using opportunities in the Matrix on the other. If you are not satisfied, you may have ignored critical information from one or other of these sources.

Saying I CHOOSE is a challenge for many people. They will try to convince you that they don't have a choice and therefore have no way to set their own priorities. They will tell you that their circumstances force them to behave in certain ways, or that others limit their options—their partner, parents, children, or their boss.

The Logosynthesis model assumes that your Essence has outlined this life for your Self, with this mission, these people, and these circumstances in this niche of the Matrix. However, from the moment you're born, the clear choice you made in Essence tends to become hijacked by the constant, overwhelming flow of information from the Matrix, as depicted in Gertrude Stein's words:[56]

> *Everybody gets so much information all day long that they lose their common sense.*

When people say I CHOOSE, they react with all kinds of thoughts, emotions, and beliefs, but a clear "Yes" is rarely a response. They start listing arguments about why they don't have a choice in this situation, or they declare their overall dependence and helplessness. Repeating I CHOOSE activates the power of words to discover your options and decide. After processing I CHOOSE, you'll recognize the deep truth of these words by Iain Thomas:[57]

> *And every day, the world will drag you by the hand, yelling, "This is important! And this is important! And this is important! You need to worry about this! And this! And this!" And each day, it's up to you to yank your hand back, put it on your heart and say, "No. This is what's important."*

21.15 Lily's reactions to I CHOOSE

Processing this statement happened quickly:

1. Does not feel true for me

2. Feeling more grounded in the statement

3. Feels true now

4. Yes! I can move on now!

If you've done deep work in processing earlier statements, later statements are usually easier to clear.

21.16 Practice I CHOOSE

Say the statement I CHOOSE. Let it sink in and observe your reactions—in your body, your thoughts, and your emotions. Write down these reactions, even if they seem silly or strange. Do this three times. You will become familiar with how you react to the statement without the added intensity of a painful issue. Then put your notes in a file.

21.17 I BELONG

Whether you stay or leave, you must connect with people. In a stable environment you may need to engage differently, while change introduces new faces. Every container in your life brings other people into your life, starting with your family and kindergarten. From there, you'll meet friends and neighbors, people at school and in higher education, employers, colleagues, clients, bosses, and members of clubs and associations. You'll meet a partner and your in-laws, and you'll form a family of your own. You belong to each of these social systems, interacting via a wide variety of roles.

21.18 Lily's reactions to I BELONG

The hard work was done in the first three statements of the Reconnect sequence. Lily needed to repeat the I BELONG statement only once:

1. Feels fine, kind of excited at the possibilities

2. Stomach butterflies like when I dive into an opening reception that's in progress

Lily's recap after tuning out from her second Move On session:

> *As I continue my open studio preparations, I am notic-ing a feeling of well-being and relaxation. It's almost shocking, how positively giddy and connected I feel. I keep trying to attribute it to the fact that I am doing less scrubbing/washing tasks, but that could not possi-bly account for this complete turnaround. My corner of the world offers a fortunate and wonderful experience.*

21.19 Practice I BELONG

Say the statement I BELONG. Let it sink in for a moment and pay attention to your reactions—in your body, your thoughts, and your emotions. Write down these reactions, even if they seem silly or strange. Do this three times. You will become familiar with how you react to the statement. Then put your notes in a file.

21.20 Fran Reconnects

Fran participated in a Logosynthesis Master Lab with a small group of experienced Practitioners in Logosynthesis. After working with me, she described her experience:

On the day I worked with Willem, I had begun suffering from severe migraines again and was really looking forward to this session. I found myself stuck and frustrated in a life full of minor and major health issues paired up with an ongoing struggle to scale my business as well as the discomfort of feeling drained by living in the house I live in. In addition to that, I also started having quite some glitches in my relationship.

Before this work, I would definitely describe my state of being as a horrible phase with no end in sight. Also, I need to share that I have been visiting many experienced doctors, naturopaths, healers, and experts to help me get out of pain and the growing anxiety around my health issues. None of the above have succeeded in bettering my state. Honestly, I was about to lose any hope that anything could help me get out of this depleting, joyless and frustrating vicious cycle.

Willem introduced me to his brand-new approach and asked me to find a symbol, color, picture, or anything that would represent my current issue(s). I immediately had a coffin show up.

Then Willem offered the statements of the Reconnect sequence, which I repeated out loud. From the first statement on I reacted strongly—from scenes and visuals to emotions and colors. With this first statement, as well as all that followed, I went into a deep state of internal work, transforming old images and memories, worries and beliefs, tapping into unpleasant emotions of anger and fear, seeing interesting visuals of amazing colors, and finally entering a state of complete agreement or at least neutrality.

After we completed this sequence, Willem asked me to go back to the image of the coffin and look at it. I was very surprised that I found a dark room and needed to imagine looking for some content with a flashlight. In the outer corner of the room, I finally found a tiny little coffin. What a transformation!

I was more than curious as to how this work could possibly lead to a transformation in my everyday reality. The first thing I noticed right after the session was that the migraine had disappeared completely. After two weeks, I can say that this work is huge. It opened me up to so many changes:

- *I calmed down around the anxiety concerning my health issues.*

- *I started sleeping better.*

- *I reclaimed my own power and strength and stopped running from doctor to doctor and from expert to expert.*

- *Lots of past emotions, often related to early experiences or to childhood conditioning popped to the surface. That wasn't pleasant, but very liberating.*

- *I managed to identify and change quite a lot of patterns that kept me stuck in a life that didn't feel aligned with who I really am.*

The work I did in this session empowered me to trust, to create and to love life again.

22

THE RELEASE
SEQUENCE

Man is born free, and everywhere he is in chains.[58]
— Jean-Jacques Rousseau

Even though you may want to move forward
in your life, you may have one foot on the brakes.
In order to be free, we must learn how to let go.
Release the hurt. Release the fear.
Refuse to entertain your old pain.
The energy it takes to hang onto the past
is holding you back from a new life.
What is it you would let go of today?[59]

— Mary Manin Morrissey

In our cheeseburger metaphor, the Release sequence is represented by the beef patty in the middle of it. Biting into it releases the full flavor of the burger—meat, vegetarian, or vegan. Releasing means letting go of anything that might keep you stuck. It's time to make room for new possibilities.

If you're stuck, your energy system is frozen in patterns that don't serve your purpose or mission—anymore. Your mind has become a museum of memories, fantasies, beliefs, and values—about the past, the future, the Matrix, and all other aspects of your life on this planet. If you become aware of this predicament, you have reached an important juncture in your life. It means that a container has fulfilled its function in the development of your Self: A child is born, a book is published, a painting is exhibited, a student receives a diploma, children have left home, or you've retired. What once was needed is not necessary anymore. You've either outgrown the milieu that nurtured you, you don't need to take care of others anymore, or you're ready for a new role within that same environment.

The Release sequence amplifies the power of Essence in your Free Self. It creates a space for the unknown, clearing the way for new patterns to emerge and allowing the power of your Essence to unfold. The statements of this sequence dissolve or release existing patterns, particularly those associated with past experiences, or beliefs that hinder your alignment with your life's mission.

This is a formidable task. People spend their entire lives creating a narrative about themselves; they tend to identify strongly with their experience, and they don't realize that any identity is relative. A confirmed bachelor can change his mind when he meets the love of his life; being married to the love of your life can be excruciating in the long run; a dream job becomes boring, and a long-desired retirement may turn into a lonely black hole. The Release sequence erodes established identities. If you have been strongly attached to a certain role and position in the Matrix, this can be shocking at first, especially in the transition between one life stage and the next, from marriage to divorce, from school to work, or from work to retirement.

22.1 The Release sequence within the Move On program

The third sequence of the Move On program is a crucial part of your journey. It can bring intense confrontations with memories, fantasies, and beliefs.

This activation may not be easy; sometimes it leads to unpleasant and even disturbing reactions that will require all your Logosynthesis knowledge to deal with.

When using Move On for personal issues, remember that all your reactions are merely energy patterns. If you don't feel calm and relaxed yet after saying a statement, repeat it. Observe changes in your emotions, thoughts, and sensations, and make notes of your experiences and reactions. If this approach doesn't work, interrupt the sequence with Time Out and then move to Tune Out. You can also follow the suggestions at the end of part III and use other techniques to neutralize emerging reactions.

If you want to work with others using this protocol, run the whole program several times on yourself or with a colleague first. It is important to have a sense of its effects, rhythm, and intensity before you guide someone else. Before the start of the protocol, you'll need to establish a firm working alliance, built on empathy, understanding, and patience. Maintain the provided structure also with your clients: When they react, ask them to repeat the statement and to describe their next reaction, until the arousal and distress subside.

A caveat: Even if you would like to know more about a reaction, don't inquire: Exploration or interpretation of an obsolete pattern will only reinforce it, not resolve it. Slow down the process and allow space for the protocol to disrupt existing associations. Once the client has returned to a calm state after completing Tune Out, you can explore what happened and discuss how they can integrate the results in their lives.

The Release sequence consists of five statements. As in the Reconnect sequence, each of these statements can trigger intense emotions and physical reactions that may require several repetitions before being fully neutralized:

1. I RELEASE THE PAST

2. I RELEASE THE FUTURE

3. I RELEASE THE MATRIX

4. I RELEASE MY SELF

5. I RELEASE MY ESSENCE

Let's explore what these statements might evoke.

22.2 I RELEASE THE PAST

If the past determines the contents of your conscious mind, nothing new will ever happen in your life. You'll remain stuck in patterns of trauma and nostalgia. You will always compare the present with what has happened, could have happened, and should have happened, but you'll never move beyond the past. I RELEASE THE PAST will free your Self from the frozen energy of past events and their influence on your current life.

This journey can be challenging, as you may find it difficult to detach from people, objects, or places that you haven't let go of yet. The statement can change nostalgia into grief as you realize that times have changed and there is no way back. The statement can also transform a trauma into a memory—it happened, but it doesn't need to determine who you are now.

The good side of this experience is that once you have lib-erated your energy system from past patterns, the freed-up energy will be at your disposal in the present. You'll need this energy to traverse the Void and shape reality.

I RELEASE THE PAST is a big one. This statement helps you clear your life energy from rigid patterns in the life you've lived up until the present moment. It contains mem-ories about how things have been, memories that made you become the person you are now. Releasing the past opens a door to exploring and realizing your potential in the now.

Initially, I RELEASE THE PAST can confront people with unfulfilled needs, wishes, and desires: Their parents should have taken better care of them, or they shouldn't have died or divorced. Also, unanswered questions arise: Why did they never get a brother or a sister? Why didn't they have more money, a better education, or a higher status in society? Objectively, all these wishes have not been fulfilled, but that doesn't stop people from holding on to them and comparing their lives with what could have been or should have been. I RELEASE THE PAST opens doors to the present.

22.3 Christopher's reactions to I RELEASE THE PAST

Christopher has long worked for an advertising company. He has gathered a lot of experience, but now it's time to leave. In the future he wants to create a profitable, sustainable marketing business. The Tune In sequence led to the image of himself walking down a street looking for the door that was his, with a trust rating of 4. I RELEASE THE PAST needed 10 iterations:

1. Resistance, shut out, closed doors and dismissal by the Matrix

2. I have a lot of experience now

3. I'm confused

4. I feel small in this new situation … even though I am not

5. I don't want to make a mistake

6. Energy shifting… Release…

7. I can live my own life

8. Others may not have released the past

9. I decide

10. One step at a time

The last reaction came in a confident, matter-of-fact voice.

22.4 Practice I RELEASE THE PAST

Say the statement I RELEASE THE PAST. Let it sink in for a moment and pay attention to your reactions—in your body, your thoughts, and your emotions. Write down these reactions, even if they seem silly or strange. Repeat these steps three times to become familiar with possible effects of the statement. Then put your notes in a file.

22.5 I RELEASE THE FUTURE

For most people we worked with, this seemed to be a strange statement—at first. If you're a responsible adult, it's a no-go to ignore the future, especially in times of expected disasters. That's true, but let's look a little bit closer, with the help of

Mark Twain:

> *I've had a lot of worries in my life, most of which never happened.*[60]

Even though I RELEASE THE FUTURE sounds completely counterintuitive, it may be a great idea to let go of fantasies about what's going to happen. Your expectations about the future may be based on a belief system that doesn't match reality anymore. Many people deeply believe that their future will be like their past, and this causes them to behave accordingly. Their habits create a continuum in which life is predictable. They're in a relationship, they get a salary, they watch Netflix, and they smoke or drink. If these habits make you happy, that's fine. However, when the patterns of your life don't satisfy you—and that's what this book is about—it makes sense to release the future. Mark Twain again:

> *If you want to change the future, you must change what you're doing in the present.*[61]

You can't let go of the future, but you can change your emotions, your thoughts, your expectations, and your fantasies about it. Releasing obsolete predictions clears your system of destructive fantasies about what will go wrong or limiting fantasies about what might go right. This pulls you back into the present and invites you to access available resources and develop your potential. And when things don't turn out the way you planned, you'll be better prepared because you can see what really exists instead of relying on limiting expectations.

It's one step to release the energy bound in representations of the past and your reactions to them. It's another step to let go of the future you've constructed based on your past experiences, especially those in childhood. The power of words in this statement may throw you straight into the Void because you have been clinging to images of the future instead of making a sober analysis of the facts.

22.6 Christopher's reactions to I RELEASE THE FUTURE

1. OK

2. It's safe to release the future

3. Calm, quiet

That was fast!

22.7 Practice I RELEASE THE FUTURE

Say the statement I RELEASE THE FUTURE. Let it sink in for a moment and pay attention to your reactions—in your body, your thoughts, and your emotions. Write down these reactions, even if they seem silly or strange. Then repeat these steps three times, so that you become familiar with possible effects of the statement. Then put your notes in a file.

22.8 I RELEASE THE MATRIX

You can't leave the Matrix, but you can let go of the energy patterns of the Matrix that you took in, that limit your autonomy. You can explore what it told you and decide if you still want to believe those things. These patterns contain all the rules, codes, and expectations that define how you should think, feel, speak, and act. At one time, these patterns may have been useful in acquiring and maintaining a status, role, or position in the Matrix to be seen or known. Now they may be limiting your Self and its potential. As you resolve those patterns, you'll be able to see the Matrix and the people in it with fresh eyes. This is especially important if you believe that the Matrix is a dangerous place where you must fight for survival, as in the short story of the lion and the gazelle:

> *Every morning in Africa, a gazelle wakes up and knows that at some point in the near future it will need to outrun the fastest lion, or it will be killed. Every morning in Africa, a lion wakes up. It knows it must be able to run faster than the slowest gazelle, or it will starve. It doesn't matter whether you're the lion or the gazelle—when the sun comes up, you'd better be ready to run.[62]*

22.9 Christopher's reactions to I RELEASE THE MATRIX

1. That's bold!

2. What is life without the Matrix?

3. Perhaps it's not about escaping but reshaping the Matrix to fit me?

4. The Matrix is there, but must define me?

5. I'm fed up with that Matrix

6. I fear a life without the Matrix

7. I appreciate the Matrix, but I won't let it suffocate me

8. Without the Matrix, every moment is new

9. The Matrix can and probably will support me

10. I've never considered this before

11. It's an intriguing thought

12. (with a smile) *Yes, that's it.*

13. It's a liberating thought too!

22.10 Practice I RELEASE THE MATRIX

Say the statement I RELEASE THE MATRIX. Let it sink in for a moment and pay attention to your reactions—in your body, your thoughts, and your emotions. Write down these reactions, even if they seem silly or strange. Then repeat these steps three times to become familiar with possible effects of the statement. Put your notes in a file for later use.

22.11 I RELEASE MY SELF

In each stage of life, you build an identity for that stage. You take on a role in the Matrix: You start as a child to your parents and a brother or sister to your siblings, you become a student, a partner, a spouse, or a parent; you're an employee, a colleague, or a boss. You separate from one partner and marry another; you move houses or places; you're self-employed, or you become a citizen of another country.

The Matrix offers countless roles to identify with, and without realizing it, your Self makes an identity out of it. You *become* that role.

For a certain period of your life, such roles may provide security, but as we said, identities are fragile because they depend on containers that are not permanent.

Identities create stability in the outside world, but once the function of a container has been fulfilled, an old identity doesn't fit anymore. When you move to a new environment, that same identity may even hinder your adaptation to the new situation. The power of words in the statement I RELEASE MY SELF disconnects you from outdated definitions of who you are and creates an open space for the possible human that you are and will be.

22.12 Christopher's reactions to I RELEASE MY SELF

1. I can show up. I can take action. I know what to do

2. I am not X, Y, or Z anymore!

3. I can talk to people ... the right people

4. I am free to do what I want to

5. My purpose radiates out from my heart, it feels so good!

6. (nods head)

7. Calm.

22.13 Practice I RELEASE MY SELF

Say the statement I RELEASE MY SELF. Let it sink in for a moment and pay attention to your reactions—in your body, your thoughts, and your emotions. Write down these reactions, even if they seem silly or strange. Then repeat these steps three times, so that you become familiar with possible effects of the statement. Then put your notes in a file. You can review them later and use them for future sessions.

22.14 I RELEASE MY ESSENCE

This statement may seem bizarre at first sight. How could you ever release the core of your own being, the deepest source of your existence in this world? Of course, you can't, but you can let go of all the words, images, and constructs your conscious mind has built around this elusive phenomenon.

Essence transcends the consciousness of your human mind. People in the Matrix have been trying to grasp, understand, and even control Essence since time immemorial—in religions, schools, communities, and cults. They have given many different names and identities this higher power: the Tao, Brahman, Spirit, Source, Essence, the Divine, the One, the Eternal, or the Force.

Some religions even banned the use of a name for something bigger than what human minds can grasp. Creation stories were written to help us understand it; prayers and rituals were designed to help us control and influence it. These concepts and rituals can stand in the way of living your Essence in the world of today.

Saying I RELEASE ESSENCE dissolves any constructs that reduce the wonder of Essence to the measure of your human mind. As a result, you'll be able to access that power from within your Self.

22.15 Christopher's reactions to
I RELEASE MY ESSENCE

Christopher needed quite some time to let this statement work because he considers himself a highly spiritual being. He was surprised when these reactions emerged:

1. Releasing my Essence? I can't do that!

2. What does my Essence really mean?

3. That's heavy, isn't it?

4. Maybe it's not about releasing but embracing Essence?

5. I'm learning to understand my Essence

6. My Essence isn't something I feel I can let go of

7. I'm letting go of the fear of losing my Essence

8. I love my Essence, just as it is. I want to keep it

9. Everyone has their own Essence, they understand that

10. I can help others find their Essence, too

11. Understanding my Essence is a journey, not a destination.

12. My Essence is always new

13. I surrender to my Essence

14. I never would have used that word before, but it feels good

15. (with a sigh) *Yes, that's it, and that's fine!*

22.16 Practice I RELEASE MY ESSENCE

Say the statement I RELEASE MY ESSENCE. Let it sink in for a moment and pay attention to your reactions—in your body, your thoughts, and your emotions. Write down these reactions, even if they seem silly or strange. Then repeat these steps three times, so that you become familiar with possible effects of the statement. Then put your notes in a file. You can review them later and use them for later sessions.

23

THE RESTART
SEQUENCE

To create one's own world in any of the arts takes courage.
— Georgia O'Keeffe[63]

And once the storm is over,
You won't remember how you made it through,
how you managed to survive.
You won't even be sure whether the storm is really over.
But one thing is certain. When you come out of the storm, you
won't be the same person who walked in.
That's what this storm's all about.
— Haruki Murakami[64]

In our cheeseburger metaphor, the Restart sequence represents the layer of delicious, melted cheese. Restart offers a new intensity to your process, an intensity of texture and flavor. Restart encourages you to embrace something new, to learn from the wisdom of your past experiences, and to continue your journey in a new way.

By working through the Reconnect and Release sequences, you have resolved a series of archaic energy patterns in your field. You have moved beyond a shell or shelter that was protecting you, you have freed the energy that was holding you in that place, and now you are ready to enter a state where it is up to you to redefine the old or shape the new. You realize that you are living in the present, the here and now, described by the well-known words of Bill Keane:[65]

Yesterday is history, tomorrow is a mystery, today is a
gift of God, which is why we call it the present.

Being in the present has its advantages:

- You make good decisions, based on relevant information.

- You feel real emotions, instead of repetitive, canned versions from the past.

- You are real, and you meet real people.

- Your actions match your mission.

Life energy bound in memories, fantasies, beliefs, values, roles, and other patterns will always interfere with your presence. The Reconnect and Release sequences clean your system like a chimney sweep. They establish the conditions for a transition from the familiar to the new, the transformation needed to enter the Land of Don't Know.

In the Restart sequence, shaping your reality becomes tangible—in an existing container or in a new one. In this sequence, you use specific statements to actively create new energy patterns that match your mission. This stage of the program unlocks your potential to take an active role in defining and determining what happens next.

The Restart sequence is where reality takes on new, concrete shapes and forms—in ways that have stretched the rational minds of many of the participants in our early Move On groups. The new reality, or the new form of the existing reality, may first appear as if it were generated more by coincidence and less by choice. The statements of the Restart sequence kindle your power to shape reality at a very deep level and in ways beyond your imagination.

Changing a container or entering a new one creates a new life—yours. Understanding how to navigate this transition is crucial for your personal and spiritual development. Most people go through life and never learn how to do this. Typical advice from the Matrix for such a transition might suggest that you find and explore your existing container or the next one, reflect on your possible roles, seek support, set realistic expectations, collect feedback, remain self-aware, and stay flexible. This sounds well thought out and logical, but something is missing. If you have ever received such advice, you know that following these steps is only possible from the present, and that past fears and traumas can interfere at any moment. That's why we refrain from giving such advice and instead activate the power of words to guide you.

Once initiated, the Move On process operates below the surface of your normal daily consciousness. You follow the instructions, say the statements, let them sink in, and surrender. From there, the words continue to work in ways that are unnoticed and beyond your control. When you make a statement and react to it, it's hard to understand how it leads to a variety of reactions, while under the surface it creates a state where your intentions shape your reality. This change affects not only you, but also others and the environment.

You can't track how a statement works, but you can trust that it will. As you practice the protocol and go through the process, you'll learn that after five, ten, twenty or even fifty iterations, you will reach a state of harmony and balance. It may require many iterations, but you will get there eventually. Sometimes you may need the support of a friend or colleague to help you stay with the structure of the protocol.

The Restart sequence consists of six statements that enable you to find your way through the fascinating Land of Don't Know:

1. I MOVE ON

2. I ENTER THE NEW

3. I CONNECT

4. I LEARN

5. I CONCEIVE

6. I SHAPE

Saying and processing the Restart statements creates a solid point of departure for leaving an existing container. You released old energy patterns of thoughts and emotions, and you have given up fantasies about the future that don't serve you. It's time to go.

You're leaving a familiar environment for the Void, the unknown. Now you exist outside of the container with all its familiar patterns, roles, rules, and resources. You're on your way to creating a new and unique shape in the world of form. This shape will make a difference; it will be the prelude to later stages of development. One book is followed by another, a painting may lead to an exhibition, a recipe to a catering event, a sporting achievement a medal, a research project to a senior position—each step contributes to the next. Each movement of your Essence into the Matrix result in more ease and skill. Now let's explore these statements:

23.1 I MOVE ON

I MOVE ON is the first step on your journey after being stuck—physically, emotionally, mentally, and spiritually. You may have met TINA in your life: the old witch who told you that There Is No Alternative. You know something must change, and that it starts with you. Saying I MOVE ON gets you moving. At first you are without a clear direction: You decide to decide. You don't know where you're going or how you're going to get there, but it's moving that matters now. This step is often the most challenging one in the Restart sequence, and it may take quite a few iterations before you feel comfortable putting one foot in front of the other. The power of words will set you in motion when you say I MOVE ON.

23.2 Lily moves on

For this session, Lily went through Tune In, and chose the image of a tiny house on the edge of a green field to represent the restriction and conflict that she felt.

1. Oh, this really hurts

2. This is so so so painful!

3. It feels dark…

4. It hurts in my chest, in my heart

5. Its so small! I can't believe I've been here so long!

6. I opened the door and shut myself inside—at the beginning

7. Its not like I just walk out of this little house, it's like I have to dig up the floors to get out

8. I don't think about it when I'm outside of it, only when I'm there

9. Is this the day I leave?

10. I'm not afraid in my head, but I am in my heart

11. The new place won't be as safe as this was

12. But it will be more exciting

13. I feel like Alice in Wonderland ... I needed the walls, but then I got too big and now it hurts

14. If I let Tom decide this, I will be as trapped as I was when I was a child

15. Its not like I don't know my new environment, I do, I've never trusted it 100%, I always had Chicago for back-up

16. I fantasized about leaving a lot, now it's real...

17. Rigid. Flexible. Rigid. Flexible. There's a choice...

18. I feel panicky in my chest. Tight...

19. It's a big deal!

20. It's an adjustment, like going to the chiropractor—it hurts for a second and then it's such a relief...

21. I'm ready, I am, I have the focus, I just need to get the timing right

22. I need to make my own security, I can do that with a plan, I'll make a plan

23. I'm sad for Tom. I don't know what he will do...

24. I do. I move on.

25. I'm ready, yes.

26. Yes I do. It feels sad but good too. Why is it so painful to move?

27. It's the old stuff that hurts, nothing new hurts me

28. It was happy, it was beautiful, it was… It was.

29. It will fade

30. I move on

31. Yes, I do. (wipes tears)

32. I move on

33. I can do both – feel the pain and move on

34. Yes, it's time (big sigh)

35. Feels settled now, feels calm. Ok

36. Yes, good.

23.3 Practice I MOVE ON

Say I MOVE ON. Let it sink in for a moment and pay attention to your reactions—in your body, your thoughts, and your emotions. Write down these reactions, even if they seem silly or strange. Then repeat these steps three times, so that you become familiar with possible effects of the statement. Then put your notes in a file.

23.4 I ENTER THE NEW

As you move on, new options will unfold and new choices appear. This doesn't mean you have to leave everything and everyone that you know behind when you enter a new world: Removing even a small pebble from your shoe can dramatically change your hiking experience. Entering the new confirms the transition, you are open to this next stage of your life. It may be as small as booking a hotel room in a city you've never been to, or as big as signing a contract for a new job, deciding to start your own business, or getting engaged.

You can only enter a new field when you move. The new is what you have never encountered before—in your perceptions, thoughts, emotions, fantasies, and memories. Your mind has a stubborn tendency to look for the known in the unknown and miss what makes the difference in this moment. If no one has ever helped you, the new will be a helping hand. If you've always been active, stepping back may offer a new perspective. If you've stayed in your office behind a computer screen, a hike in green surroundings may bring about the change you need to solve the problem at hand.

23.5 Lily enters the New

1. It's not new

2. Its new to be alone, to be free

3. I'm not what or who I was … no way!

4. I might be alone but I am not diminished … that's interesting!

5. Lots of doors in front of me…

6. I'll do what resonates, I won't do them all at once

7. Each day is new

8. I've been looking at it like its one huge event, but I can do little new things one at a time! (laughs)

9. New things are like treasure, so if I'm finding new things each day, as I go, then it becomes a treasure hunt…

10. It just needs to matter to me, not the whole world

11. Everything I create … meetings, calls, ideas … they are all treasures for me to collect as I go

12. This is exciting!!! (laughs) *I can't believe I'm even saying this!*

13. I can do this. I can. No, I WILL!

14. Yes. I. will.

23.6 Practice I ENTER THE NEW

Say the statement I ENTER THE NEW and let it sink in for a moment. Pay attention to your reactions—in your body, your thoughts, and your emotions. Write down these reactions, even if they seem silly or strange. Then repeat these steps three times, so that you become familiar with possible effects of the statement. Then put your notes in a file.

23.7 I CONNECT

You may not know the land, but you're aware that your Essence has brought you here. You know you're not alone. When you have lost a loved one or were fired from a great job, the world may seem like a lonely place to you. You've left your old container, and you've entered another one. Your first task in this new environment is to become familiar with this new world and the people in it. On the first day of my writing retreat in Grenoble, where I wrote this chapter, I checked into the hotel where I had booked a room for nine days. The man at the desk was friendly, as were all the other members of the hotel staff. I didn't know the city, so I explored it in widening circles to get a feel for its character. I found restaurants that I liked and went back to them several times. After a few days, people began to recognize me with a smile.

23.8 Lily connects

1. I see a spider in a web, busy going between all the important points

2. The better I connect, the less the disconnect will hurt

3. I can make an effort to make new connections, dedicate time

4. I mustn't overload myself … that's important

5. I'm not starting from scratch

6. I'm not alone, it's a network, and I'm a networker

7. Its about resonating again, isn't it?

8. I have power here, I have something people want

9. I'm not afraid, I know inside me that I can do this

10. I am important enough

11. Yes. I connect.

12. I connect. (nods and smiles)

23.9 Practice I CONNECT

Say the statement I CONNECT. Let it sink in for a moment and pay attention to your reactions—in your body, your thoughts, and your emotions. Write down these reactions, even if they seem silly or strange. Then repeat these steps three times, so that you become familiar with possible effects of the statement. Then put your notes in a file.

23.10 I LEARN

To become acquainted with the Land of Don't Know, you will need to learn. What are the points of interest? Which language do people speak? How do they meet, greet, and make decisions? What's off limits in this new corner of the Matrix? A few years ago, I was invited to offer a keynote address at a Canadian conference. After the Chair welcomed the attendees, they suddenly all stood up and began to sing a song that was unknown to me. It turned out to be "Oh Canada," their national anthem.[66] I was completely confused, and it took me at least a minute to grasp that I was expected to stand up with my hand on my heart. I LEARN opens your mind to acquire new information without embarrassment or anxiety, and creates a new frame of reference that will serve you on the path to fulfilling the mission you came here for.

23.11 Lily learns

1. Who I really am. Just me, with no one else

2. A new way to live in the world

3. New things

4. How to

5. Art, history, and math (laughs)

6. To do new things

7. That I am ok … even if I cry about it

8. What to do next?

9. When, how, what, and why

10. Everything I need to know, because the universe tells me

11. From life

12. And will be wise

13. That this too, shall pass

14. I learn me

15. Everything I need to know

16. Where I belong

17. Beautiful things

18. To protect myself

19. That I am

20. Yes. I learn. It's taken me a long time!

21. I learn. It feels so serene…(eyes closed, smiling)

23.12 Practice I LEARN

Say the statement I LEARN. Let it sink in for a moment and pay attention to your reactions—in your body, your thoughts, and your emotions. Write down these reactions, even if they seem silly or strange. Then repeat these steps three times, so that you become familiar with possible effects of the statement. Then put your notes in a file.

23.13 I CONCEIVE

Once you have either re-examined the codes, rules, and laws of your familiar environment, or you've explored and become acquainted with the new environment, fresh options appear. You become more aware of your mission because you're no longer overwhelmed by overwhelming stimuli from the Matrix. You begin to focus, perceive, and recognize new resources and opportunities. You use them to develop new ideas, your ideas. It's time to conceive: Something new is happening, something never seen before will emerge, and it's you who provides the container for that. This is different from receiving; receiving is when the source of the new is outside of your Self.

Conceiving is based on more than body and mind: It's the result of a free interaction of the energy of your Essence with your resources in the Matrix, your external environment. At first, the result of I CONCEIVE may seem random because you met this person, saw that movie, or read this book. If you look closer, you'll see a dance happening between your Essence and the Matrix. This dance is a unique combination and expression of Essence with available resources: The Matrix mirrors and displays to you what has happened. Initially, your ideas have no immediate effects on reality, but you may start to think about designing the forms, structures, and patterns of how you want to shape that reality—your reality.

23.14 Lily conceives

1. That's a pregnant word!

2. Miniscule to fully grown

3. Conception is fascinating....too small to see, so life-changing

4. 172 ideas! (laughs)

5. Conceive … perceive … it's not the same…

6. That if I stay on track, I will be OK

7. I don't know what I have conceived, I won't know until I see it

8. If I conceive it, that means it's mine

9. I am responsible for it

10. What if I mess up?

11. Conceiving is scary! I feel anxious now, I don't know why though

12. It's not just me, it would be me and whatever I created

13. Tightness in my chest, heart is pounding

14. I don't like this!

15. A little better

16. I want it to be ok

17. I have conceived already. Making it happen is the birth

18. I am further along than I thought

19. I can conceive whenever I want to, need to

20. I feel strong. Creative. Powerful. Wow!

21. I always could do this, but I didn't know

22. This is what I do, how I make my art

22. This is who I am!

23. Yes!

23.15 Practice I CONCEIVE

Say the statement I CONCEIVE. Let it sink in for a moment and pay attention to your reactions—in your body, your thoughts, and your emotions. Write down these reactions, even if they seem silly or strange. Then repeat these steps three times, so that you become familiar with possible effects of the statement. Then put your notes in a file. You can review them later and use them for future sessions.

23.16 I SHAPE

You have arrived in the next container, you have learned and practiced everything you needed, you have planned and tested your ideas and concepts, and now it's time to act. For real. It may be an activity in the Matrix, like inviting people for dinner, publishing an article, showing a painting, or performing your song or composition. It may be another kind of visible action or decision, like moving to a new place, finding a new job, or marrying your partner. You can start by dipping your toe in the water, feeling if it's still too hot, and pulling it back if necessary. You may test your plans within your circle of friends or your wider network to get feedback from them, fine-tuning your ideas and strategies. Your friends' reactions will help you decide whether to step back and review your plans, or whether to move forward.

The statements of the Restart sequence often lead to elation, joy, surprise, curiosity, or an eagerness to start a new project or meet new people. When you have completed all six statements of the Restart sequence, move to Tune Out. Often the Tune Out sequence continues to provide a wealth of additional ideas and thoughts about possible next steps.

23.17 Lily shapes

1. An image of wet clay on a potter's wheel, mess

2. It doesn't look like anything yet

3. Hands are fascinating, your whole life is in your hands

4. They shape the clay with pressure, pressure shapes…

5. Warm hands

6. It gets worse before it gets better

7. Its so hard if you don't learn how when you're younger, still makes me sad

8. Maybe the mess is ok, part of it somehow…

9. What shape?

10. My life now

11. This life now

12. New things, I create a perspective

13. I shape how I want to

14. I'm curious

15. Maybe that's where I went wrong, I didn't shape, I let everyone else do it

16. Ship shape

17. Beautiful things

18. How the hands hold

19. I can apply pressure and respond to it

20. Two-way street

21. I like this

22. This is weird, weird but easy somewhere inside (smiling)

23. Where my feet walk

24. Hands and feet, like shapes left in the cement

25. I will leave my mark

26. (looks up and nods)

23.18 Practice I SHAPE

Say the statement I SHAPE. Let it sink in for a moment and pay attention to your reactions—in your body, your thoughts, and your emotions. Write down these reactions, even if they seem silly or strange. Then repeat these steps three times, so that you become familiar with possible effects of the statement. Then put your notes in a file. You can review them later and use them for future sessions.

23.19 Lily's journey continues

About two months later, we heard from Lily. She had been busy since her last session, but she was frustrated and confused: She told us that she had recently moved her newer art and some equipment into her studio in Chicago, she was spending more time there. She had also been offered two solo shows—though not in Chicago or in commercial galleries. One had great facilities and many interesting exhibition spaces. However, she decided against this option because she was advised by members of her community who had negative experiences with this gallery. The other opportunity was from an exhibition center in Miami that had previously not been promising in terms of opportunities and sales—the curator now offered her a solo show.

Lily was disappointed, saying "These are so far from what I hoped for. I wonder if it's worth the time and effort—and the forced time away from Chicago."

She also told us that she had recently been rejected from a lucrative opportunity in Washington to have some work included in a prestigious art collection. She thought it was in the bag, and she had been left processing the shock. She said, "I want to contribute, and I also wanted to be paid! Things just aren't working out… I am attempting to find the meeting point between my mission and the opportunities that are available to me."

It was sad for us to see how Lily hadn't managed to connect to the life force within her Self, even after working with the Move On program for a longer time. She needs the security of her Illinois home and hasn't found the resources she will need to succeed as an artist in the challenging environment of the Chicago art industry.

Lily's example illustrates how a safe container can inhibit the courage to act, even when that safety doesn't make you happy. The Void can offer a harsh confrontation with painful early experiences that keep you from living your full power. In such a situation it's crucial to seek professional help, and Lily did that. The Move On process had brought her existential dilemma between freedom and security to the surface, and she realized she needed professional assistance to help her find a new perspective that will enable her to meet the Void. Lily is continuing her process with her therapist. This can take considerable time.

The Move On program may trigger a wide variety of emotional and physical reactions, some of which can be painful or even overwhelming. To slow down the process, to reduce its intensity, or to temporarily interrupt it, we created *Time Out*. This is a series of three statements that gives you the opportunity to become grounded again, recover a little, and start again when you're ready to.

You can use Time Out if a reaction is still intense after 10 or 20 iterations, at which point you need a breather. You can also insert it after running each of the Reconnect, Release, and Restart sequences, to allow your system to integrate what happened during the last sequence.

Time Out consists of three short statements:

- I BREATHE

- I REST

- I AM HERE

You say each statement and as usual, let the words do the work. Concentrate on taking slow deep breaths as you say these Time Out statements. This interlude softens the more dramatic effects of the Move On program. Repeat each statement as many times as necessary.

24. Anna needs Time Out

In her first session, Anna had Tuned In and began the Reconnect sequence. After two statements she became very anxious and began to panic because an old memory came up. The Practitioner immediately moved to Time Out to create some space, and here are Anna's responses:

I BREATHE

- *I feel quite panicky! Is this normal?*

- *I don't like it!*

- *I'm OK, I'm OK…* (breathing faster)

- *OK, that's better, feeling better*

- *I'm alright*

- *I'm OK* (calm voice, normal breathing)

I REST

- *Oh…*

- *Yes, that's nice…*

- *It's good to rest*

- *Rest…*

- *Yes, I rest*

I AM HERE

- *That feels strong*

- *That's what matters now*

- *I don't need to do it all now*

- *I'm not alone*

- *I really am*

- *I… AM… HERE…*

- *Yes, I am here…*

- *That's a relief!*

24.2 Practice Time Out

Check your inner state at this moment: thoughts, emotions, and physical sensations. Then say the following statements, let them sink in and work for you, then repeat them until the distress fades:

- I BREATHE

- I REST

- I AM HERE

What happens when you do this?

We have already mentioned that your experiences with and reactions to the Move On program will be quite different from previous applications of the Logosynthesis model. It sometimes seems more like a bumpy ride on a rollercoaster when compared to the gentle, quiet steps of the Basic Procedure. The program initiates deep changes in fields where you didn't realize there could ever even be a problem.

One participant in our Move On class wrote that she felt "thrown backwards" as far as losing the gains from what seemed like years of personal development. In fact, she had repressed or covered up deeper layers of pain and childhood trauma from those years. The Move On program urged her to address these issues, which she didn't appreciate at first.

The fact that issues are addressed at such a deep level means that the long-term effects of the Move On program are quite different compared to the Logosynthesis Basic Procedure. The latter offers an endless gamut of applications for every disturbing perception, memory, fantasy, or belief; it can offer relief for each of them. One of our colleagues even refers to it as a "toothbrush for the soul," a daily routine to clean up your system and help you to focus on what's relevant.

In contrast, the Move On program changes your entire Self in its dynamic interaction with your Essence and the Matrix. After dealing with everything that is activated by the statements of each sequence, you reach a new level of awareness. The issue you start with can potentially be treated and resolved with any of the other Logosynthesis techniques. However, if the issue keeps coming back in myriad forms, it makes sense to explore that issue at a deeper level. Doing so may open Pandora's box: You are suddenly confronted with vast areas of frozen patterns you didn't even know existed. If you choose to run the program, such a wealth of unexpected insights can be overwhelming. Move On is not a rose garden, so take your time and get support from a family member, friend, or professional if you feel insecure or anxious.

Once you get deep into the process, after hundreds of iterations of the statements over a period of weeks or months, you'll notice that things change. YOU become different. Your body posture and your energy level change, your emotions begin to vibrate at a higher frequency, shifting from guilt, shame, and fear to confidence and courage. Your thoughts change from being repetitive and ruminating about minor issues to seeing the bigger picture of your mission in the Matrix. New actions follow these new thoughts.

Big things can happen, such that we've learned to not underestimate the impact and power of these simple statements: One participant realized she needed to end her long-term relationship in order to continue growing. Chloe ended her contract and moved laterally in her profession; another person realized that it was time to address an area of major trauma in his life.

Another, even more surprising effect is the changes you observe in the Matrix. Suddenly, doors open where you used to bump into walls, and the Matrix becomes friendly in unexpected ways, providing chances you never dared to dream of.

Old friends reappear after many years, business opportunities present themselves unsolicited and free of charge, your credit score shoots up without explanation, and you attract the generosity of strangers.

Another effect of the repeated statements is a change in the way your mind works. Each single statement becomes a part of your frame of reference in coping with daily troubles. For example, someone criticizes you, and I TRUST pops up; you're reminded of an unpleasant event of the past, and I RELEASE THE PAST appears immediately. The statements all cover different aspects of your existence, and this helps you to stay in the present. Your mind will increasingly become aware of this over the weeks and months that you use the Move On program.

Persistent loops of ruminating thoughts are short-circuited by the statements. In the beginning, you'll remember and recognize the statements when they appear. Eventually, they fade into the background of your mind and from there, they'll perform their functions, keeping you stable and focused on what's important.

MOVE ON AND OTHER
LOGOSYNTHESIS TECHNIQUES

26.1 Why use other techniques?

As we developed the Move On program and experimented with its use, we found that it was sometimes useful—and relatively easy—to combine elements of the Move On program with other Logosynthesis protocols. There are reasons for doing this:

■ It deepens your process: The Move On program can take a long time. You may be on a roll with the statements and then suddenly a disturbing memory or belief surfaces while processing. It is not directly related to the symbol or metaphor that you have chosen, and to get past it, you can use either the Basic Procedure or the Lego Protocol from *Alone to Alive*. This allows you to quickly neutralize the painful memory or belief in this way and continue on your journey.

■ It minimizes distress: Repeating the Move On statements can sometimes activate distressing emotions and physical states. Normally, you can reduce these reactions by repeating the statement the second you feel uncomfortable. There is no need to suffer or prolong it; just repeat the statement, and let it sink in again. However, if the pressure remains uncomfortable, you can also switch to the Basic Procedure. The Basic Procedure is familiar to most people who know Logosynthesis and provides an additional layer of safety when material is particularly distressing.

■ It allows you to work intuitively: Move On Is an intuitive program. It has a distinct structure and within that structure you are free to experiment and explore according to your needs, your available time, and your preferences for techniques and protocols. Move On is meant to allow you to go with your flow and work intuitively.

26.2 Which techniques to use?

The most effective protocols to combine are the Logosynthesis Basic Procedure, Lego, and Bricks. A summary of the Basic Procedure can be found in chapter 34 in the Appendix of this book and a full description with many examples in *Discover Logosynthesis*®. Bricks and Lego are described in *Alone to Alive*. If you have taken Logosynthesis training, you can also use other techniques such as Mapping, Timelines, Metaphors, or the Simonton Protocol.

27

THE COURAGE

In my life I have found two things
of priceless worth – learning and loving.
Nothing else, not fame, not power,
not achievement for its own sake
can possibly have the same lasting value.
For when your life is over,
if you can say "I have learned" and "I have loved"
you will also be able to say "I have been happy."
— Arthur C. Clarke[67]

You've moved on; you've taken a different path. You don't know what made you do it, and you don't know how. Looking back, it was a roller coaster ride, unpredictable in its twists and sudden movements, but once you found the courage to create, the tunnel came to an end and gave way to a wide and open space. With F. Scott Peck you took the road less traveled, and that made all the difference. Courage means doing what you've never done before. No one else can do what is yours, and in a state of courage, you surrender to that destiny.

In the Move On process, the first full cycle of the protocol is the most challenging one. Sometimes it seems like there is no end to it, as new aspects emerge with each iteration of a statement. It feels like surfing waves of intense emotions, somewhere between mad, sad, glad, and scared, before gliding onto a shore of relief and relaxation. As you continue the program and repeat the sequences, you begin to notice sparks of insight. You know why the past happened, why you're here now, and why you created this possible future; your mission from Essence designed your destiny, but your Self made the path towards fulfillment—by walking.

In subsequent rounds of the program, after the first cycle, certain statements will take on new meaning. The same Reconnect sequence that activated deep old pain can make you feel lighthearted, evoking a big YES, each time. YES, I AM! YES, I KNOW! In later rounds, other aspects of your past and your future may come to the fore.

Also, the Void becomes different. Its character changes from threatening to almost soothing, a place where you can be and explore what's coming up for you, now, in the niche you've chosen in the Matrix for your most personal endeavor. You finally experience what it means to go placidly amid the noise and haste; you're understanding the Stoics who have told you that the world is as it is, and that it's only your reaction that can be changed. As you run the program, a new You begins to unfold: a human being, not a human feeling, a human thinking, or a human doing. Some patterns were there long before the current issues appeared on your path, and they are not relevant to the person you are now.

Once the program becomes part of your journey, a new way of using the protocols emerges. Instead of saying and processing all statements of all sequences, you become aware of a particular sequence or a single statement that you need to go through now. It will start when you encounter a new challenge. You explore, zoom in, and focus without being overwhelmed. You know you are, you know, you trust, you choose, and you belong, so you just say I RECONNECT. You know it's time to let go of the past, the future, and all frozen aspects of the Matrix, your Self, and what you thought was Essence, so you say I RELEASE, and you will let go of whatever is in the way. Then you move on and explore what's relevant now, whom to meet, what to learn, and how to act, all in the service of your mission.

In this way, Move On becomes a strategy for navigating your way through life. It becomes more effective with practice because your ability to separate the wheat from the chaff increases. Once you've internalized the program, you won't even need Reconnect or Release because you'll connect and let go whenever it's needed. Sometimes, single statements from the protocol will flash up in your mind, and you know you need a few repetitions of I KNOW because you had temporarily forgotten *that* you know, or you need to release the future after a wave of bad news has flooded your mind.

The world won't stop moving you. Here my intelligent spell checker insisted on its own version: "The world won't stop loving you," and yes, that was our most important discovery in writing this book. Not everybody loves you, and you don't have to love everybody; that's not why you're here. You're here for your X, to create a form in which you can grow and develop, and in which others can grow with you—shaping reality in a friendly container—together.

That's where you will find the ultimate form of the courage to create: *the courage to be.*

As you gain experience with the Move On program, you'll notice that strange things start to happen. These things seem to be related to your original assessment of the issue, but in completely irrational ways. This phenomenon can provide completely unexpected ideas or solutions coming from the Matrix, as in the following experience:

On the feast of All Saints, November 1, 2022, I was in Grenoble for a week to work on this book. After a full day of writing and editing, I went for a walk in the city. I passed by a church and saw that its doors were open; the interior was brightly lit, and I went inside. The service was ending, but the choir was still singing, and the fragrance of incense pervaded the air. I stood there for a while, listening to the music. As I turned to leave, a woman handed me a piece of paper with the name of a saint written on it. It said "Saint François de Sales." I had heard of this saint in my Catholic upbringing and knew that he founded an order of monks known as the Salesians but I didn't know anything else about the holy man. Back in my hotel room, I googled the name, and was deeply touched by what I read:

> *To live Salesian means to live in the presence of the loving God in everything I do, and to do it in a kind, winning, positive, cordial way, so that the people I meet do not get the impression that this life in the presence of God is a burden to me or makes me sick and depressed, but this life in the presence of God gives me life in fullness, today as well as after my death.*

Living Salesian also means being a Christian in everyday life, embodying small virtues: humility, meekness, patience, cordiality, optimism. St. Francis of Sales is guided by the word of the biblical Creator to the living things of the world, they should bear fruit, each according to its kind (Gen 1:11). Each is called to bear its fruit. A bishop cannot and should not live like a monk. Spouses not like Capuchins, nor craftsmen like cthe ontemplative religious, praying half the day. But all fruits God wants, each according to its own kind. Francis de Sales created a new unity between profession and religion.

This was written 400 years ago, and very fully aligns with my teachings. In other words, stay in contact with Essence, discover your mission, and carry it out into the world.

The Tao that can be told is not the eternal Tao;
The name that can be named is not the eternal name.
The Nameless is the origin of Heaven and Earth;
The Named is the mother of all things.
Lao Tzu[68]

I want to beg you, as much as I can, (…)
to be patient toward all that is unsolved
in your heart and to try to love the questions
themselves like locked rooms and like books
that are written in a very foreign tongue.
Do not now seek the answers,
which cannot be given you because
you would not be able to live them.
And the point is, to live everything.
Live the questions now.
Perhaps you will then gradually,
without noticing it, live along some
distant day into the answer.[69]
— Rainer Maria Rilke

This book has not been easy for us to write, and it may not be easy for you to read, for the same reason. Many paragraphs and pages are packed with words and sentences that invite you to explore troubling memories, fearful fantasies, and limiting beliefs. Along the way you may make discoveries that touch you more than you ever expected. We had experiences of being constantly distracted, losing focus, and getting lost, with deep doubts as to whether what we were doing made sense.

At times we were overwhelmed by our own discoveries, and we had long discussions about the ethics of this endeavor. Finally, we concluded that our discoveries and experiences had opened so many doors for ourselves that we didn't want to deny you, dear reader, the opportunity to open such doors in your own life.

It's in the nature of shaping reality that you must rise to a certain frequency in order to get things done. This frequency is fostered by approaching things with loving compassion. Unfortunately, in the Move On process, there is no way to bypass the things that you have covered up in the past. They all have to be be looked at thoroughly.

You can overcome these limitations—not by always looking at the bright side of life, but by facing them and discovering that they're not real, that they're nothing but dark energy patterns that fade away in the daylight of direct attention.

Speaking single statements in the protocol may hurt. However, only by going through multiple iterations will you discover that such reactions never come from your Free Self. They come from pockets of your mind filled with past pain or future disaster. Speaking the statements will empty those pockets and create a space for life in the present.

Shaping reality doesn't come from making plans. Making plans comes from shaping reality. Reality emerges from a deep awareness of what's next in this life, with these people and with these tasks, in this place.

May the light of your soul guide you;
May the light of your soul bless the work you do
with the secret love and warmth of your heart;
May you see in what you do the beauty of your own soul;
May the sacredness of your work bring healing,
light and renewal to those who work with you
and to those who see and receive your work;
May your work never weary you;
May it release within you wellsprings of refreshment,
inspiration and excitement;
May you be present in what you do.
May you never become lost in the bland absences;
May the day never burden;
May dawn find you awake and alert,
approaching your new day with dreams,
possibilities, and promises;
May evening find you gracious and fulfilled;
May you go into the night blessed, sheltered, and protected; May
your soul calm, console and renew you.
— John O'Donohue[70]

APPENDIX

This Appendix contains the following chapters:

31 OVERVIEW OF THE MOVE ON PROTOCOL

This chapter offers an overview of the five sequences of the Move On protocol.[71]

31.1 Tune In

The steps of the Tune In sequence:

1. Pick an issue.

2. Assess your trust level that this issue can be resolved on a scale 1-10.

3. Say I EXPLORE, let it sink in, observe, and make notes. Say this **three** times.

4. Say I ZOOM IN, let it sink in, observe, and make notes. Say this **twice**.

5. Say I FOCUS, let it sink in, observe, and make notes. Say this **once**.

6. Find a word, a perception, a metaphor, or a symbol for what you found and make a note or a drawing.

31.2 Reconnect

Say each of the following statements, let them sink in, observe, and make notes of your reactions to the statement. Repeat each statement until you reach a state of calm, relaxation, curiosity, and joy:

1. I AM

2. I KNOW

3. I TRUST

4. I CHOOSE

5. I BELONG

If you reach a state of calm after processing all five statements in the first session, move to Tune Out. If any statement in the Reconnect sequence leads to high distress after many iterations, you can take a Time Out (see below). If a Time Out reduces your distress level, you can continue. If it doesn't, move to Tune Out. You can also run the Logosynthesis Basic Procedure for the statement that got you stuck.

31.3 Release

In the second session, you repeat Tune In and Reconnect. Then move to the Release sequence. Say each of the following statements, let them sink in, observe, and make notes of your reactions to the statement. Repeat each statement until you reach a state of calm, relaxation, curiosity, and joy. The statements of the Release sequence:

1. I RELEASE THE PAST

2. I RELEASE THE FUTURE

3. I RELEASE THE MATRIX

4. I RELEASE MY SELF

5. I RELEASE MY ESSENCE

If you reach a state of calm after working through all statements of Reconnect and Release in the second session, move to Tune Out. If any statement leads to high distress after many iterations, take a Time Out. If this reduces the distress level, you can continue. If it doesn't, move to Tune Out.

31.4 Restart

In the third session, you repeat Tune In, Reconnect, and Release. Then move to the Restart sequence. The statements of the Restart sequence:

1. I MOVE ON

2. I ENTER THE NEW

3. I CONNECT

4. I LEARN

5. I CONCEIVE

6. I SHAPE

If you reach a state of calm after working through all the statements of Reconnect, Release, and Restart, move to Tune Out. Take a Time Out if necessary.

31.5 Tune Out

You can move to Tune Out any time as described above. In the Tune Out sequence, you go through the following steps:

1. Remember your word, perception, metaphor, or symbol

2. Examine what happened to it in the process

3. Return to the original issue you picked

4. Examine what happened to this issue

5. Reassess your trust level 1-10

6. Envision your future regarding this issue

7. Leave the room, rest, relax and drink water

31.6 Time Out

Time Out does what its name implies. It allows you to take a break when the work is demanding. It makes the overall experience of the program smoother and easier. Running the program is sometimes thorny, and it's important to know how to pace yourself when it is.

Time Out gives you a pause and a rest during your session. The combination of the three statements slows down your process or interrupts it for the moment. You can recover a bit and continue when you are ready to go again.

You can use Time Out whenever a reaction is still over-whelming after 10 or 20 cycles of saying a statement, letting it sink in, and taking notes. You can also insert it after running any of the Reconnect, Release, and Restart sequences, to give your system time to integrate what happened in each sequence.

Time Out consists of three statements:

- I BREATHE

- I REST

- I AM HERE

You say each statement and let the words do the work, while you focus on taking slow, deep breaths. Repeat each of the Time Out statements as many times as you need. Drinking water will help to keep your energy flowing.

31.7 Remember to drink water

Drinking water improves the flow of energy throughout the body and supports your work with any Logosynthesis protocol. A steady flow of energy makes it easier for you to process your experiences. Staying well hydrated stabilizes and maximizes the benefits of each session. If you do all the above and are still having difficulty, take a Time Out or switch to Tune Out and stop working for the day. If you find the work overwhelming and still too difficult, work with a partner or a professional. There is no need to struggle or suffer.

Cathy is a certified Practitioner and Instructor in Logosynthesis, and she is following the curriculum to become a Master Practitioner. She has published two books about her learning and experiences in applying the model, and she fulfills a variety of roles within LIA, the Logosynthesis International Association. At the time of writing, she has just enthusiastically accepted a position on the Board of Trustees. She is highly motivated to bring Logosynthesis to the world, with a focus on people in senior leadership positions. This chapter describes Cathy's application of the Move On program, which she completed over a number of sessions. The issue she chose to work on was the fact that her own Logosynthesis training/mentoring business was not yet sustainable. Her initial trust level for this issue was 3 to 4.

32.1 Tune In

In this sequence, the following reactions to the statements show up:

I EXPLORE:

- *I must narrow it and I don't want it to do that*

- *People aren't necessarily enthusiastic at this point*

- *There is more focus on the I now*

I ZOOM IN:

- *Letting go of resistance if others don't want to explore*

- *Shifting from resonating with others to what I can do instead*

I FOCUS:

- *Acting with others, meeting them where they're at*

When she translates this focus into an image, she visualizes a table with people around it. From there she begins the Reconnect sequence.

32.2 Reconnect

I AM:

1. Tightness in throat area

2. Throat shoulders tension

3. Tension in my head

4. It moves down in my body

5. Feels calmer.

6. I'm not so concerned about what others think and say. I don't have to react to it

7. I can choose my words

8. Joy sitting around the table

I KNOW:

1. You know

2. Very competent in knowing

3. I have a sense I don't need to know it all. I know something inside, confidence. What I know will serve me well

4. An element of listening to others

5. (Shaking her head left to right, up down)

*6. I bought Iain McGilchrist's book "The Matter with Things."
Put all in the context of what I already know. Curiosity. Inner
knowing.*

7. Let go

*8. I use writing to put a context around what I know. Do I need
to do that or is that just part of letting go?*

9. Am I trying to prove? Do I need to prove it or not?

10. Words come up: Just let it be.

*11. The table with the people comes up, just let it be. People will
know you know*

12. Stay curious and listen

I TRUST:

1. I'm in a safe place to trust

2. I'm surrounded by a presence that makes it safe to trust

*3. Sometimes my impatience gets in the way of trusting. I don't
know if that's trust*

4. Tension in the back of my neck

5. I sense I'm a little sad. Why does it have to be so challenging?

6. Sadness is still there

7. Still sadness, but I have a sense that people mean well

8. Pause. That sadness is ebbing. I'm not doing this on my own. We're in this together

9. I can't make other people trust

10. I don't have to make other people trust. If I can trust, calmer, create a safer space

11. I'm in a good spot to trust. I have what I need to trust

12. (Nods) It just is. I trust

I CHOOSE:

1. I have to choose something different than what's being discussed at the table

2. I choose to embrace something for my well-being. I expect other people to choose the same challenge

3. It's not easy. Those could be my mother's words.

4. I have learned it doesn't have to be so hard

5. I was very comfortable engaging in conversation at the table. Why did I decide to change my conversation?

6. Tension in my shoulders. Conversations were intensive. There is a different way to have these conversations

7. It doesn't have to be one or the other. I can have these conversations

8. I choose to continue moving forward. I'm not having the conversation I want to have. I am moving

I BELONG:

1. I have strong connections and a big family. I belong even though some may not resonate. Belong to the table but not have a voice around the table

2. A little bit of a headache, a loud table I belong to

3. Long pause. There is something coming up around family with smart people and everyone being right. Energy put into being right. I can belong without being right. I can let go

4. More of sense of being in the belonging. Just be

5. Calmer. I don't have to prove anything to belong.

6. I am where I am

The Reconnect sequence of the first session ends here. She has reached a state of calm in reaction to each of the statements. We move to Turn Out to close the session.

32.3 Tune Out

On moving back to the image of the group of people, Cathy says that she feels more joyous if she allows the people at the table to be as they are. The Reconnect sequence has made room for lighter feelings. People are themselves and she doesn't need to push or pull anyone. Her trust level has risen to 7-8, without emotion or tension:

> *I don't need to trigger a reaction from them, I can speak from my heart*

After this session, I sent Cathy the instructions for follow-up sessions, adding the Release sequence.

32.4 Cathy's next steps

After her live online session with me, Cathy ran the protocol herself on several consecutive days. On some days, she just Tuned In and stayed with the Reconnect sequence, on other days she added the Release sequence after Tune In and Reconnect. The following report comes from one of those sessions.

The Tune In sequence

The issue remained the same:
I want to create a profitable, sustainable business.

I EXPLORE:

- *Networks and connections*
- *Customers and audience*
- *Warm and cold audiences*

I ZOOM IN:

- *Show … don't tell*
- *Meet them where they are*

I FOCUS:

- *Prevention and growth*

She translated what showed up after I FOCUS into an image of a seed growing where it's planted.

Her trust level for this image was a 4 on a scale 1-10.

The Reconnect sequence

I AM

1. I am here

2. I grew here but it could have been easier … more flow

3. I would have liked that but would have needed someone to hold space for me

4. I'll create a microclimate

5. How can I enhance growing conditions?

6. Not recognized/understood

7. People are looking for different conditions

8. Think energy

9. Life energy

10. Don't make assumptions

11. Energy

12. My energy is frozen in finding 'right' language to attract an audience in Nova Scotia / Canada

13. Doing this

14. Current thinking: Is something wrong with your brain?

15. Think energy

16. Find an audience interested in energy

17. Change the dialogue

18. One part of the whole

19. A necessary part for our times

20. Peace. Love. Joy.

21. Too comfortable

22. Here

I KNOW

1. A model to share with others

2. Skeptics

3. Be patient. Create space

4. Celebrate

5. Think energy

6. Exciting

7. Keep going

8. Stay grounded in your knowing

9. Calm

I TRUST

1. OK. I trust

2. Seeds can withstand a lot and flourish in better conditions

3. Find a connection point for people

4. Go for emotions

5. That's not me. I like facts

6. OK go for facts … with an open heart

7. Kindness and compassion

8. Calm

I CHOOSE

1. I want to do this

2. Struggle with so many options for further education

3. How I show up in the Matrix

4. Reflecting back on my choices. I could have done so much more but then I wouldn't be here now

5. Be conscious about your choices going forward

6. What do you want to transform? Leadership? Healthcare?

7. What is your legacy?

8. Book I gave to Trudeau … he chose

9. Individual. Matrix

10. Plant seeds

11. Calm

I BELONG

1. Essence in the Matrix

2. Self-Awareness

3. OK

32.5 Adding the Release sequence

I RELEASE THE PAST

1. Resistance and dismissal when in the Matrix

2. I now have experiences

3. Energy bound in words

4. With kindness and compassion

5. Notice the energy of words. Choose high energy words

6. Release. Pain. Suffering. Guilt.

7. Be open and creative for new ways

8. Others may not be open yet

9. Show them how to release memories or pressure

10. One step

I RELEASE THE FUTURE

1. OK

2. Safe to release future

3. Calm

I RELEASE THE MATRIX

1. Let it fall away

2. Yawn and stretch

3. OK

I RELEASE MY SELF

1. I can show up. I don't have to stand off

2. Release reactions towards others in order to hold space for them

3. Speak

4. Beyond family and friends. Beyond Logosynthesis community

5. Radiate out from heart. Empowering

6. Shaking head

7. Calm

I RELEASE ESSENCE

1. Why should I do that?

2. That's me!

3. Wow, now I get it…

4. Yes, I understand

5. Relief, calm

Tune Out

The energy is different now … still planted in the same place but thriving now!

Cathy's level of trust at the end of this session is a 7 on the scale of 1-10.

32.6 Cathy's adds the Restart sequence

Tune In

The issue: I want to create a profitable, sustainable business.

I EXPLORE:

- I can do this
- Shake head. Focus
- Don't overthink it

I ZOOM IN:

- *Where to start? You've already started*
- *Put yourself out there… too comfortable here*

I FOCUS:

- *People want to hear from you*

When she translates this focus into an image or a movie:

- *Me talking to an audience and people listening / coming to hear me.*

Her level of trust is 4 on the scale 1-10, with a comment: Be articulate and authentic; don't show off. From there she begins the Reconnect sequence.

The Reconnect sequence:

I AM

1. Calm

2. Don't have to prove anything. Listen to others

3. Calm

4. Calm for several more iterations

I KNOW

1. Ask for help

2. Calm for several iterations

I TRUST

1. Don't worry if people listen or not, understand or not

2. Calm. You don't need to control where the message goes. Put it out there

3. Calm. How beautiful!

I CHOOSE

1. I chose a long time ago. 'What holds you back?'

2. I am doing the best I can where I am right now

3. 'Don't underestimate the power of your choices to date'

4. 'Thank you for choosing. Be confident to continue moving forward'

5. Articulate it

6. You're doing well with your choices

7. Don't underestimate your influence

8. Bravo

9. Exciting. Joyful. Hopeful.

I BELONG

1. I do belong. (A beautiful family wedding this past weekend!)

2. I can be me and we each can be

3. I know how to release limitations and restrictions

4. It's a beautiful place to belong

5. Feels good. Calm

The Release sequence

I RELEASE THE PAST

1. A lot of beliefs and memories. I know they're energy

2. Jaw shifting. Head shaking back and forth

3. When I was as supportive as I could have been (let go of guilt I could have done more/better)

4. It is the past. Experience

5. Calm. Acceptance

6. Calm

I RELEASE THE FUTURE

1. Business is based on what I do now

2. Give some space to build a big container for business

3. Relax. Allow. Accept.

4. Let others help. Not all about doing for others

5. Calm

I RELEASE THE MATRIX

1. Fully immersed but not attached

2. Action. Grow the almond

3. Let go of tension

4. Supportive

5. Content exactly where I am. Room to grow

I RELEASE MY SELF

1. Allow. Expansive breaths

2. Exactly where I am meant to be

3. Calm. Deep breaths

4. Be kind and compassionate

5. Sense of shedding layers. Self stepping forward

I RELEASE ESSENCE

- *OK to speak of it*

- *True to my Self. True to the work and what it is*

- *It's safe. It's beautiful*

- *I don't need to hide behind layers*

- *Calm, sleepy*

Adding the Restart sequence

I MOVE ON

1. Step outside comfortable container knowing I'll always belong

2. Can offer and receive support even if not physically present all the time. I have been noticing this lately

3. Bigger than my family and Logosynthesis community

4. Step into new communities with grace and presence

5. Support by my current communities

6. Shape a new business container not to please but what's needed

7. I know reactions won't always be pleasant. OK, I can step into something new knowing I'm supported. That was important part to build foundation for business

8. Structure. Clarity of vision with room for unknown

9. I'm ready after the wedding this weekend because I know we're all supported

10. Exciting

11. (Smiling) *Ready*

I ENTER THE NEW

1. Here I come!

2. Proactive. Not reactive

3. Choose your words. Focus your voice. Presence

4. I have been entering the new but not finding open doors and open arms

5. Knock. Respect. Listen. Culture.

6. With kindness and compassion. Love

I CONNECT

1. Know what to say and how to say it. Trust.

2. Gentle knowing

3. With respect, kindness, compassion, grace, love, patience

4. From the heart. Listen to others

I LEARN

1. Listen to what they want

2. Don't push

3. Left and right hemispheres

4. I'm curious to keep learning!

I CONCEIVE

1. I have been conceiving for the past five years

2. Content and Theme are the same but need connections

3. Pain behind right ear. Sit with it

4. Shape it based on what I know and others too

5. That has always been my strength at work

6. I know how to do this on my own and with others

7. I've enjoyed a lot of time conceiving already

8. Now I have to act

I SHAPE

- *Package it for my business*

- *Don't doubt yourself*

- *Different packages for different people*

- *Tingling higher in my head*

- *Allow*

Tune Out:

After she returned to her focus and the original issue, Cathy wrote:

> *Speaking and presenting specific messages to specific audiences with one overall message for all. Speaking to their ears. Hope. Kindness. Compassion. You are enough. Your personality is not you – you are so much more. Finding the space to choose. From self-talk to inner voice of Essence.*

Her level of trust was now an 8.

32.7 Cathy's conclusion after ten sessions

Cathy seeks to create a profitable, sustainable business by teaching others how to use Logosynthesis as a healthy life-style practice. Cathy recognizes many potential benefits for people working in organizations who struggle with demanding workloads, multiple priorities, and challenging relationships. She recognizes that she is not converting her desired target audience due to several factors: Successful professionals may not recognize the need; Logosynthesis is not yet established nor recognized as a solution; her product positioning needs to be refined and results proven. In addition, there is still, at the time of this writing, there is still resistance and dismissal of this innovative model.

Cathy recognizes that her energy is blocked in various aspects of creating a new container for her desired business. She is interested in using the Move On program to resolve these blocks to gain awareness for her mission and to clarify goals for her company. Over the course of ten self-coaching sessions using the Program, she recognized certain patterns:

▪ Energy was bound up and limiting her ability to clarify whether she was really committed to starting a business, especially since she was already quite comfortable in her current lifestyle.

▪ She developed a desire to explore and go wide rather than narrowing her work to a specific target audience.

▪ She gained the insight that she has already been incubating the business over the past several years.

▪ She began to better understand the challenge of creating the container on her own versus leading a team or collaborating.

▪ She begins to appreciate a strong sense of connection to her family field, both siblings and ancestors.

▪ She discovered subtle physical responses associated with facial and throat areas, relating to the quality of her voice.

- The images she focused on were consistently related to individuals in organizations.

- There was a sense of releasing the resistance she was experiencing from others, and with that, she gained clarity to move forward with her goals.

It took Cathy ten sessions to complete the Move On protocol. At the end of these sessions, Cathy sat with the above content that she had documented. As she did this, she began to recognize her responsibility in creating this business; and felt that by doing so, it would empower individuals to create a healthier lifestyle in a rapidly changing world. She realized how much she is already supported in the larger container of her family field. And she realized that she still has some resistance to narrowing her target audience and creating her own container in the Matrix. However, she is committed to moving forward with more ease and flow, with more kindness and compassion. She feels better able to allow herself (her Self) to show up in her interactions with others and to meet people where they are.

LOGOSYNTHESIS AS A MODEL
FOR HEALING AND DEVELOPMENT

Logosynthesis.
Words relieve the aching heart,
Path to inner peace.

This chapter offers an overview of the most important concepts of Logosynthesis theory and provides the basics of some techniques as they are used in self-coaching and professional guidance. I will also provide some case examples.

33.1 Introduction

Logosynthesis is a model that assists people in mental and emotional healing as well as in walking their path of personal and spiritual development. I discovered the model in 2005, and it has been expanding ever since. Logosynthesis is derived from many 20th century schools of counseling and psychotherapy. As a newer branch on the rapidly growing tree of energy psychology, Logosynthesis helps people to find and fulfill their life's mission, with the help of the ancient power of words, a century of psychoanalytic wisdom, and the latest insights of neuroscience. The model is also deeply rooted in humanistic psychology and in a spiritual understanding of human existence.

Logosynthesis assumes that every human being is a manifestation of Essence, which can also be thought of as one's Higher Self, immortal soul, or spirit. We also assume that human beings have a task, purpose, or a mission in this existence—to explore, to discover, to learn, to practice, to teach or to contribute to the consciousness of the universe as a whole. Upon entering the world of form, a human being is a coherent system of energy in flow, which we refer to as the Original Self.

The Original Self is equipped with a body and a mind as instruments in the service of its mission. The body is the hardware, the vehicle that allows a newly born human to explore their physical environment through their senses. After a period of growth and learning, the body becomes a sophisticated vehicle that can proactively act and react to the environment. To function properly, the body needs food, water, shelter, movement, rest, and practice. If these conditions are not adequately provided, the body will goes into *survival mode* and take control, suppressing signals from the mind and from the Higher Self, from Essence. In survival mode, it responds to perceived threats with fight, flight, freeze or fawn.

The mind can manage complex situations and corresponds with the software of this vehicle. When it's operating in *competence mode*, it allows the person to fulfill physical, psychological, social, and cultural needs and desires, based on planning and strategy. The mind has a wide range of options that it uses to influence and react to the environment in the service of needs and wants. It allows the person to understand other people and objects in the environment and to build a frame of reference from which the body perceives and acts. The mind also has needs: Information, consistency, variety, attention, support, and respect. When these are not provided, the mind takes over and tries to create situations in which these needs are fulfilled. When this happens, the accomplishment of a person's mission from Essence fades into the background of the subconscious mind.

Body and mind support the mission of the Original Self when their needs are met. Otherwise, they get in the way of the task of the Original Self. When the person is in contact with their mission, their thoughts, emotions, and actions are guided by the requirements of that mission in life. If the needs associated with certain stages of development are not sufficiently met, the development of the Self is arrested, and the awareness of body and mind can usurp the awareness of the Self's true nature and mission. This is known as trauma.

33.2 Life energy

Energy is the ability to affect something. It is needed to accelerate a body, heat a substance, create an electric current, or emit electromagnetic waves. Plants, animals, and humans need energy to live. Energy can flow freely or be stored, for example, as food, oil, or in a reservoir in the mountains.

Energy exists in many forms, as physical energy as described above, but also as matter, information, and consciousness. In Logosynthesis we understand energy as the creative force of Essence, the energy of life. This is not new: Aristotle referred to the concept of *physis*, a force of growth in nature that causes organisms to develop into higher forms—embryos to grow into adults, and healthy people to work toward their ideals. Different cultures have different names for this force:

the Egyptians had the concept of Ka, Indian tradition has Prana, and the Chinese call it Qi. Even the scientific concept of evolution may be a well-disguised version of this force.

Many biologists and psychologists are skeptical of the concept of life energy. Freud called the idea of a universal creative force in nature "a pleasant illusion," and Rudolf Virchow wrote in the 19th century:

> *Medical science (...) has proved that life is merely an expression of a sum of phenomena, every single one of which occurs by known physical laws.*

Eric Berne, the founder of transactional analysis, eloquently stayed out of the discussion:[72]

> *Perhaps physis (life energy) does not exist at all, but despite our inability to be definite about this subject, there are so many things which happen as if there were such a force that it is easier to understand human beings if we suppose that physis does exist.*

Energy psychology—and therefore Logosynthesis—takes a different approach: It assumes the existence of an all-encompassing life energy that gives meaning, and then makes this energy its basic operating principle.

33.3 Energy patterns

In the Logosynthesis model, life energy is either flowing or bound up in energy patterns. When life energy is not in flow, when it's still waiting to be activated, then we consider it to be frozen or organized in different patterns. All your static perceptions, ideas, feelings, emotions, and thoughts are patterned energy that can block or obstruct the flow of our life energy and keep you stuck. In this world, you need a balance between flowing and structured energy to be able to orient yourself. If too much of your life energy is in flow, our mind becomes chaotic and overwhelmed. Conversely, if too much of your energy is still, or even frozen, you cannot act and react appropriately. People and events on your life path affect this balance. Energy patterns can be supportive or limiting. Supportive structures act as beacons of stability and groundedness in the sea of impressions and events in your daily life. On the other hand, limiting structures create problems because they restrict your orientation to the bigger picture, and generate inadequate reactions.

33.4 The space-time continuum

In Logosynthesis, we assume that frozen energy patterns exist in a space-time continuum, just as tables and chairs have a place in your living room at a certain moment in time. If you take a photograph of these objects, you freeze that moment in a picture. If a life experience is overwhelming, you can freeze that moment as an energy pattern in your internal personal space, similar to having taken a picture with your camera.

You can see, hear, sense, smell, or even taste these energy patterns. They are 'in your mind's eye.' If you take a moment to think of your parents, you may remember the expression on their faces, you might hear your father's voice or feel the arms of your mother around you. Every perception of a person, object, or event in your life can create an energy pattern in your space-time field. The combination of all these structures offers a map that enables you to find your way in life. This map may be incomplete, with blank areas, or incorrect with wrong routes; or it can be a finely detailed representation of the outside world.

Energy patterns can influence you most powerfully if they exist in your body or in your immediate vicinity, i.e., within your personal space. These energetic structures can be threatening or stimulating, and thus you react to them with many different emotions. A memory of a beloved person can lead to joy or grief, depending on the location of that person in space and time. The voice of a person you don't like, held in your energy field, can lead to anger or fear, even if the actual person is a thousand miles away.

During and after traumatic events, parts of the energy of the Original Self will get split off and freeze as separate energy patterns; this is what causes disturbing memories. A girl who has been abused will carry the frozen images, sounds, and body perceptions of the experience in her space-time field. These energy patterns contain a limited form of consciousness, locked in the moment of the trauma, and they are disconnected from the awareness of the Original Self and its corresponding Essence. The frozen consciousness in these structures can be reactivated in response to similar or associated events.

If a person's boss behaves in the same way their angry father behaved, the person will experience the same emotions they felt in the original traumatic event with their father. Because this reactivation can be extremely painful, the Self creates defense mechanisms, another form of energy pattern, to protect the Self against re-experiencing the trauma. After multiple traumatic events, a considerable amount of the person's life energy can be frozen in memories, fantasies, and beliefs. The Adult Self is what's left of the Original Self after these events.

33.5 Restoring the flow of life energy

Our task as facilitators of change and development is to restore the flow of energy through the frozen patterns in order to heal the fragmented Self, to make it whole again. Logosynthesis works via the client's redirection of their energy to the Free Self, with connections to Essence and in concert with their mission in the Matrix. It resolves the deepest cause of suffering, which is our disconnection from Essence. This disconnection results from the reactivation of traumatic memories along with their corresponding fantasies and limiting beliefs. Therefore, our job is to first diagnose the traumatic experiences that have led people astray from the path of the Original Self. Once we have a diagnosis, we can begin to resolve the mechanisms the person has developed to avoid the pain.

Logosynthesis work empowers people to retrieve the energy of split-off parts and restore the flow of life energy. Such parts can be stuck in the past, but they can also cause you to compulsively focus on the future. As part of this body of knowledge that comprises Logosynthesis, people can also learn to remove the energy of adopted or introjected values, beliefs, emotions, and behavioral patterns from their energy system and personal space; returning it to where the pattern initially came from, and where it will no longer cause harm. This allows the true or Free Self, the unique person, to emerge.

For all this to happen, you must realize that most of your emotions, beliefs and thoughts are nothing but frozen thought forms that we perceive as real, and that we keep re-activating. The first step towards healing is to retrieve your own energy from an event or situation. This disconnects you from the associated symptoms, emotions, or beliefs. In a second step, you return the energy of others that are also involved in the situation or experience back to where it belongs, so that it's no longer frozen and causing symptoms. In the third and final step, you retrieve your energy from your emotional reactions to the event, further separating you from the consequences of it. This is done by using the power of words. Here is an example:

33.6 The case of Sarah: resolving stage fright

Sarah is a 35-year-old business coach who used to get anxious when she had to play the piano in front of other people. Within minutes, she was able to resolve this issue with the help of Logosynthesis. I asked her to imagine the situation in which she experienced the fear, and then guided her through the steps of the Logosynthesis Basic Procedure:

Sarah: *I watch myself playing the piano, getting all tense.*

She receives a sentence:

I retrieve all my energy bound up in this image of myself playing the piano, and I take it to the right place in my Self.

Sarah repeats the sentence and stays silent for a while:

I become a bit calmer.

She receives a second sentence:

I remove all non-me energy related to this image of myself playing the piano, from all my cells, my body, and my personal space, and I send it to where it truly belongs.

Sarah repeats the sentence and again stays silent for a while:

I become sad and cannot play anymore.

She receives a third sentence:

I retrieve all my energy, bound up in all my reactions to this image of myself playing the piano, and I take it to the right place in my Self.

Then, after a long silence, Sarah says:

I'm playing music, not notes!

33.7 The power of words

Sarah's case illustrates how Logosynthesis uses the healing and manifesting power of spoken words to dissolve emotional blocks and limitations. The more frozen patterns are released, the more our Essence shines through. Compared to the fields of psychotherapy, counseling, and coaching, what we are doing here is a revolution. Traditionally, professionals use words to reflect the client's experience, to find a description for the experience, and to interpret it. Here we do more than that: We use specific words to create therapeutic change. There are many precedents for this in spiritual traditions, and in fact throughout history we find many examples of creative and magical acts performed through the intentional use of words. In these traditions, creation, healing, and magic all take place through the use of words as a *manifesting force* in itself, without the need for further explanation:

■ And God said, "Let there be light!" and there was light.

■ Jesus said to the crippled man, "Rise, take up your bed, and walk." At once the man was healed, and he took up his bed and walked.

■ Abracadabra, derived from the Aramaic words ארבדכ ארבא (avr ah ka dabra): *"I create as I speak."*

Traditional counseling and psychotherapeutic models tend to remain in the realm of biology and psychology. They do not apply the spoken word for its ability to heal and manifest. Language is used as an instrument to describe reality and to indirectly influence the client's world—through conditioning, interpretation, trance, anchoring, and cognitive reframing.

Logosynthesis offers specific formats to access the manifesting power of words. This power is then used to dissolve destructive thought forms, and the energy bound up in them becomes immediately available for the person in the here and now. This healing goes to the core: The release of frozen energy patterns allows the Free Self to emerge and express itself.

Logosynthesis has a tangible effect. After a successful intervention, the atmosphere in the room changes. It seems to become quiet in a special way: The traffic sounds less intrusive, the birdsong stronger. Normally, the symptoms the client works with do not return. However, new aspects of dissociated parts may come to the surface of conscious awareness to be dealt with.

33.8 The Logosynthesis Basic Procedure

Logosynthesis methods follow certain patterns, which in time can become a ritual. Its Basic Procedure consists of several steps which can be used in both self-coaching as well as under the guidance of a professional. The examples below have been formulated for the self-coaching mode, but they're also valid in working with clients. Professional guidance has the advantage that the client can feel much safer in accessing traumatic memories and phobic fantasies: They are not alone. In a solid working alliance, the client won't be distracted by the details of the procedure and can fully concentrate on the processing of the accessed memories, fantasies, and beliefs.[73]

For the sake of clarity in this chapter, I have chosen to limit my focus to the processing of a disturbing image or voice in a concrete situation. As you will learn from the case reports, this is only one example of how the Logosynthesis Basic Procedure is used. The *Logosynthesis Handbook* offers a wide range of options in the application of Logosynthesis to memories (trauma), fantasies (phobias) and limiting beliefs. In the next chapter, you will find a detailed description of the Logosynthesis Basic Procedure. A more comprehensive version has been described in my book *Discover Logosynthesis®*.

33.9 The application of Logosynthesis in self-coaching

For people who are emotionally and mentally stable, Logosynthesis is an excellent way to resolve everyday challenges in the workplace, in relationships, and in coping with health and money issues. It's relatively easy to learn the procedure in one-day workshops as offered by Logosynthesis Instructors, or from my 2015 self-coaching book.[74] You can use Logosynthesis to prepare presentations or difficult meetings, to deal with disturbing events in daily life, or to view tasks from a more rational perspective.

It's common for people to struggle with Logosynthesis when they first use it. With practice, the sentences will flow more easily and self-coaching becomes routine. The more energy the method releases, the easier it becomes to face traumatic experiences and recognize frozen energy patterns.

However, there are limits to the self-application of Logosynthesis. Even though people wish they could resolve everything themselves, as soon as traumatic events from a person's past get in the way of rational coping with people and circumstances, we recommend to seek the support of a trained professional. Such a guide can offer a working alliance that puts the client's issues into perspective and allows the person to face and resolve traumatic experiences. In the past few years, the training and certification of professionals has received top priority in the Logosynthesis International Association.

Logosynthesis self-coaching can also play a role in the ongoing guidance by a coach, a counselor, or a psychotherapist. If a firm working alliance has been established and the client has worked through several issues with the help of the Logosynthesis Basic Procedure, the guide may teach the procedure to the client and encourage them to use it for smaller issues, leaving the more emotionally charged themes for the sessions with the professional. Once the client has learned that the sentences work, they will gain self-confidence in practicing the Basic Procedure. In this way, the autonomy and independence of the client will continuously increase, and the frequency of the sessions can be reduced to a minimum, to process the issues the client can't cope with on their own.

33.10 The application of Logosynthesis in coaching and counseling

Professionals in coaching and counseling tend to focus their attention on finding solutions to life's problems. The boundaries between those disciplines and psychotherapy are not easily drawn, but in general we can say that psychotherapy is more focused on the treatment of mental disorders and their roots in the patient's history. Coaching is more commonly used to address workplace issues, while counseling is directed towards finding ways to cope with life's challenges in finding meaning, overcoming transitions in various life stages, and creating mutually supportive relationships.

Logosynthesis applications can play an important role in each of these disciplines. It's important to stay within the respective boundaries of the professional's scope of practice, even though the ease, speed, and elegance of Logosynthesis might invite one to cross those boundaries. Coaches and counselors can run into professional problems if their management of boundaries is fuzzy. Therefore, I recommend the following approach for the use of Logosynthesis in coaching and counseling:

▪ Take enough time to build a deep, stable working alliance. Doing so will make the client feel safe and secure with you if old, repressed material starts to emerge. This will also protect you against the tendency to use the sentences too early. Always build trust and rapport first before using the sentences.

▪ Avoid clinical diagnoses in your work: Trauma, anxiety disorder, phobia, etc. You don't need these terms in the

application of Logosynthesis and they might even stand in the way of the process. It's enough to know if and where energy is blocked or frozen, and to identify the character and degree of distress of the blockage found.

- In coaching and counseling, you can stay with very simple categories for energy patterns. For the representations of objects, it's most important to explore whether they are visual, auditory, kinesthetic/tactile, olfactory, or gustatory (VAKOG); in your work with reactions, you must explore if these are structured as physical, emotional, cognitive, or behavioral.

- As a coach or counselor, you start from the issue presented by the client and remain close to the client. You refrain from interpreting any possible source of the presented symptoms and you don't explicitly ask for childhood experiences. A counseling intervention might be: "Have you experienced this before?" while a psychotherapeutic intervention would be: "When and with whom did you experience this before?"

- In coaching and counseling, you concentrate on the identification and dissolution of beliefs and fantasies instead memories of traumatic events.

- When clearing triggers, address people in the client's current life and use general formulations in the sentences—like "This representation of X and everything it represents." The past will then be neutralized without being directly activated.

- Always stay three steps behind the client. Don't push them or introduce your own images and interpretations. Staying behind them guarantees that no disturbing experiences will be unnecessarily or prematurely activated. It also stabilizes the working relationship.

- During the exploration, ensure that you return regularly to the presenting problem of the client. A link will then remain between the client's conscious reason for seeing you and the process initiated by the sequence of sentences.

- Avoid using the sentences for any emotion or psychological concept: Think of the triggers and reactions as being manifestations of frozen energy and focus on representations of sensory experiences.

- The use of images and metaphors as issues for the sentences also allows for resolution without directly activating disturbing events. Avoid your own metaphors and use those that have the most emotional emphasis for the client as the content for the sentences.

33.11 The case of Pierre: neutralizing distressing expectations

Pierre is a young man with Crohn's disease who volunteered for a recorded video session. He regularly needed to undergo colonoscopies and contacted me because he kept postponing the appointment for this uncomfortable examination. The last one had been done five years earlier and he was overdue for another procedure. In the initial interview it turned out that Pierre's resistance was not related to the examination itself, which was done under anesthesia, but rather to the tedious preparation for it. This involved drinking liters of an unpleasantly smelling bowel prep solution. He also feared the repetition of an earlier situation where he threw up the contents of a few bottles of this fluid, after which he had to start all over again. This session with Pierre provides a good example of the use of Logosynthesis in a counseling session, which stayed within the boundaries described above.

When Pierre imagined his preparation for the colonoscopy, his distress level was extremely high, a 10 on the 0-10 scale. In the application of the Logosynthesis Basic Procedure, Pierre went through the neutralization of a whole range of perceptual triggers, i.e.:

- The terrible taste of the saline solution he had to drink.

- The pink color of the saline solution in the bottles.

- The visual markers on the bottles, which signified how much he had to drink each 15 minutes.

- The smell of the saline solution in his nose.

- The kinesthetic experience of his stomach almost exploding from the fluid.

- The image of himself vomiting a wave of the liquid.

After applying several rounds of sentences on the above triggers, Pierre's feet felt warm, and he perceived the colors in the room more intensively. When I asked him to imagine making an doctor's appointment and going through the preparations, we needed a final round on the image of the monitor and the colonoscopy tube in the examination room. Then he said: "I feel tired now, I'm going to sleep while they're going to do the procedure." It turned out that the procedure itself was associated with a deep feeling of relaxation due to the effects of the anesthesia.

33.12 The case of Alexander: smoking cessation

On the second day of a three-day training seminar, Alexander presented his desire to stop smoking. We had agreed the night before to work on this issue, and he hadn't smoked since then, so he was experiencing an intense craving. Alexander had been smoking on and off for years and had recently started up again. When I asked him *why* he smoked, he answered that he felt a need to do it. This 'need' showed up as a feeling in his chest, a 'sucking force.' I asked him if he really believed that this force indicated the need to smoke a cigarette, and Alexander confirmed that it did. I told him that I had my doubts about that hypothesis, and carefully took him back in time to the first time he'd felt this sucking force.

He remembered a situation as a seven-year-old, in the hospital, during which time he had felt abandoned: His parents weren't there. He reported that this was the first time he had this sensation, and this had happened long before he had ever touched a cigarette. When I went further back with him, another memory showed up from when he was four years old. In this memory, he woke up from anesthesia after surgery, and also in this memory no one was there, and his throat felt dry. Alexander neutralized this memory with the help of the sentences of the Logosynthesis Basic Procedure; after that he felt a great relief. Then I took him back to the situation in the hospital when he was seven years old, and he saw himself standing at the door of the room, waiting for his mother. After two rounds with sentence 1, this image was gone.

The intensity of the symptom in his chest had decreased, but it hadn't disappeared yet. Since this was a demonstration, there was a time limit and I had to finish. I gave him a last round for 'the hidden perception that leads to this feeling in my chest 'and then' the sucking force' went away.

Alexander learned in a deep, experiential way that the symptom in his chest didn't mean that he needed a cigarette. The feeling was actually associated with a traumatic event in early childhood that was occasionally reactivated. Smoking a cigarette made the feeling disappear—but only for a limited amount of time. Nicotine needs only 10 seconds to reach the brain and soothe a memory. In this case, the Logosynthesis intervention took 30 seconds to peel off a layer of the under-lying traumatic pattern. Alexander now prefers to practice the latter.

During the lunch break after the session, there was no need to smoke a cigarette. In the future, Alexander still has some homework to do because other adverse childhood experiences may show up. He was hospitalized four times as a child, and the addressed events probably weren't his only experiences of being abandoned.

I often see a connection between early experiences of abandonment and addictive behavior. When we manage to access these traumatic events and neutralize them, the need for substances and actions to manage the painful state tends to decrease in intensity.

33.13 The case of Laura: overcoming a fear in a car

Laura presented with a phobia of traveling by car—riding for long distances in a car with her husband caused her to panic. She said, "I feel trapped," and the idea that there were no farms or other buildings for miles made her feel extremely anxious. When I went back in time with her to the origin of this anxiety, it had been there all her life, even at birth.

As I guided Laura through pregnancy, the fear was not there during her first three months in the womb. What must have happened after that time? She recounted the story of a car accident that her parents were involved in. It was in the fourth month of Lara's time in the womb. The car was wrecked, nobody was badly hurt, but mother was in shock.

When we said the Logosynthesis sentences on behalf of Lara's mother, there was enormous relief, with deep sighs, especially after the second sentence. On returning to the memory of the womb, Lara then switched immediately to the time of her birth and said "I'm trapped!": These were the exact words she had used for her experience in the car. At the time of birth she had been literally trapped, with her delivery taking more than 24 hours because of a breech presentation.

When we said the sentences for Lara's perception of the body of her mother during birth, there was again a deep relief. When I asked her to visualize the upcoming long journey in the car with her husband, she started to smile and said: "I'm looking forward to our holidays!"

33.14 Logosynthesis Training for professionals

Logosynthesis' potential reaches far beyond the scope of this chapter. The Basic Procedure is relatively easy to learn, but the professional application of the model with clients requires previous education in coaching, counseling, or psychotherapy, as well as advanced training in Logosynthesis.

Trainees engage in intense learning and personal work that gently questions the concepts and methods they have previously used, before transferring what's learnt to the situation they're working in. Also central to the Practitioner curriculum is the awareness that any client can activate the personal history of any professional. The limits of what your clients can achieve will always be determined by your own limits. Your development and the unfolding of your Essence in a professional context are therefore key goals of the program.

The Logosynthesis International Association sets standards for the content and structure of the training program. Certification training is offered as for Practitioners, Instructors, Master Practitioners, and Trainers in Logosynthesis. The

Association also informs the public about Logosynthesis in general, explains the training programs in more depth, maintains a list of certified professionals, and runs the website www.logosynthesis.international.

34

THE BASIC PROCEDURE:
A SUMMARY

This chapter describes the Basic Procedure of Logosynthe-sis from the vantage point of a professional working with a client.[75] If you're applying it on your own, find a quiet spot in a comfortable environment with enough time for the work. If you don't feel safe enough to address challenging issues, find a professional to support you.[76] If you're already familiar with Logosynthesis methods, then you know the procedure always follows a similar path:

▪ If you're working with someone else, you always want to establish a solid working alliance first. You must reach a level of trust necessary for the person to be willing to leave their comfort zone and embark on a journey into uncharted territory. Your clients need to know they're in good hands and that the tools and techniques you use will help them on their life path. Therefore, you must build up a level of trust that allows your client to accept your way of working in the same way that they might trust their family dentist or car mechanic.

▪ Once your client feels welcome, you begin to explore the reasons why they have come to you and create a space to let them share their story. This is a precious moment for many people; they meet you in moments of pain and tend to feel profound relief when someone really listens.

▪ As they are talking, begin to listen for cues to use in the next step of the treatment. How does the client describe the world they live in? How big are the powers and influences they are experiencing? Are they able to think clearly, or are they caught in memories, fantasies, and beliefs? Which emotions show up, and how do they influence the client's behavior?

▪ Once the client is comfortable, you start to explore what is behind the image of the world as the client perceives it. What is triggering emotions and physical responses? What is in the present and what is hidden in their history? What are fantasies about the future? You carefully guide a transition from the presented issue to a world not yet explored.

▪ Next, you determine the level of distress the client is experiencing in relation to the presented issue, and you move from listening to the story to exploring essential aspects: Which people, times, and places were significant in the early stages of this distress? Many complaints that seem to be firmly rooted in the present are in fact deeply rooted in a painful past.

▪ Once you have identified which frozen perception is causing the client's distressing reaction, design the content for a cycle of the three sentences of the Basic Procedure for that trigger. Offer the sentences only if the client is open to your methods. This openness is located somewhere between dependence and resistance: If a client is completely dependent on you, they are probably too reluctant to take responsibility for themselves; if they're resistant, they won't allow the sentences to work as intended.

▪ Each sentence contains a label for the trigger you will process together. This label represents a memory, a fantasy, or a belief, and uses words that refer to a perception: Most often, clients see a person, hear a voice, sense the touch of a person, or they notice a smell or a taste.

▪ The label rarely contains an emotion or a reaction to a perception. For many professionals, this may be unusual because traditional models tend to focus more on emotional reactions than on the perception of the events that trigger those reactions. Use the client's own wording for the label.

▪ Before you continue, ensure that the client has a glass of water ready. It often happens that clients begin to feel tired, dizzy, or nauseous when they start the work. These sensations are usually an indication of intense processing and they disappear when the client drinks water.

▪ When the client is ready for a step into the unknown, you offer them the first sentence and ask them to repeat it.

▪ You give the sentences in small chunks, a few words at a time—this is not a memorization test. You let the client repeat each part and take the time to allow each sentence to sink in. With experience, you'll recognize the signs that the sentence has finished working and will then offer the next one. The first sentence is:

> *I retrieve all my energy, bound up in (this perception), and I take it to the right place in my Self.*

You give that sentence in parts and invite the client to repeat each part after you. The first time may feel unfamiliar, but in fact, it's not much different from a family physician asking a patient to say "Ah."

▪ After the client has said the sentence, there is a working pause to process the information given to their system by the sentence. In this pause, different reactions are possible, from yawning, muscle contractions, and relaxation to the surfacing of deep emotions. If emotions arise, repeat the sentence with the client, being careful not interrupt the cycle with discussion.

- The same procedure is applied to the second sentence:

> *I remove all non-me energy, related to (this perception),*
> *from all my cells, all my body and my personal space,*
> *and I send it to where it truly belongs.*

This sentence is also followed by a working pause.

- The third sentence follows the same pattern:

> *I retrieve all my energy,*
> *bound up in all my reactions to (this perception),*
> *and I take it to the right place in my Self.*

Allow enough time to let the words sink in, especially after this third sentence

- After the cycle of three sentences and their working pauses, invite the client to share their experience, usually with the help of an open-ended question such as, "What's happening now?" This will reveal whether the presenting issue has been resolved or whether additional exploration and sentences are needed.

- When the distress level is sufficiently reduced and nothing new comes up, the next step in the Basic Procedure is *future pacing*. You invite the client to imagine their future to determine if the distress they were experiencing has disappeared. If it has not, begin a new cycle, focusing on the issue that arose in the future pacing.

- If everything is resolved and the future pacing is no longer causing distress, you have the option of closing the cycle or exploring what else needs to be done in the session.

- The more you work with Logosynthesis on your own issues or with clients, the easier it becomes to apply the Basic Procedure. There are endless possible variations, but they can all be reduced to the steps above.

- For many Logosynthesis trainees it is a continuous challenge to let go of skills and knowledge they already have in coaching, counseling, and psychotherapy. In Logosynthesis it is rarely necessary to linger with intense emotions: The search for the trigger of these emotions and its neutralization will bring faster relief than the most empathic form of staying with them.

- There is also no need to interpret events or to offer a new frame of reference to help the client understand what is happening in their life or how to enact change. Once the power of words has done its work, many clients are well equipped to come to this new understanding on their own—to their surprise and to mine.

- If you'd like to get a feel for the Logosynthesis Basic Procedure, you'll find a wealth of applications on our YouTube channel, *The Origin of Logosynthesis*®, with playlists in different languages.[77]

35.1 Dr. Willem Lammers

Willem (1950) studied social and clinical psychology in the Netherlands. He holds a doctorate in psychotherapy from Middlesex University in London. After graduation, he gained initial experience as an assistant professor at the Medical Faculty of the Free University of Amsterdam. Preferring clinical practice to an academic career, he accepted a position in Davos (CH) at a high-altitude rehabilitation hospital, where was involved in both patient care and management. After becoming self-employed, he founded and ran a training institute for coaching, consulting, and organizational consultancy in Switzerland for many years.

Since the beginning of his career, Willem has worked intensively at the boundaries of body, mind, and spirit. He is trained in Bioenergetics, Transactional Analysis, Hypnotherapy, Gestalt Therapy, NLP, and various modalities of Energy Psychology. In 2005 he discovered the principles of Logosynthesis and has been constantly developing the theory and methods of this amazing model ever since. He founded the first Institute for Logosynthesis, designed a training curriculum for professionals working with Logosynthesis, and assisted in the founding of the Logosynthesis International Association.

Willem has published eleven books in six languages and regularly publishes articles and essays. He runs his own practice and teaches in Switzerland and internationally.

You can reach Willem through his website:
https://willem.lammers.ch/write01

Books by Willem Lammers

These books are the best way to get acquainted with Logosynthesis as a model for healing and development:

■ Lammers, Willem (2020). *Discover Logosynthesis®. The Power of Words in Healing and Development.* (Logosynthesis Light Series). Also available in Dutch, French, German, and Italian.

An introduction to Logosynthesis as a system for self-coaching:

■ Lammers, Willem (2015). *Self-Coaching with Logosynthesis®.* CreateSpace/KDP. Also published in German, Serbian, and Italian.

Logosynthesis for people who work with people:

■ Lammers, Willem (2015). *Logosynthesis® Handbook for the Helping Professions.* CreateSpace/KDP. Also available in German and Dutch.

The other books of the Logosynthesis Live series:

■ Lammers, Willem (2019). *Minute Miracles. The Practice of Logosynthesis®. Inspiration from Real Life.* Also available in Dutch, German, and Italian.

- Lammers, Willem (2020). *Reclaiming Your Energy from Your Emotions: States of the Mind in Logosynthesis®*.

- Lammers, Willem (2020). *Sparks at Dawn: Awakening with Logosynthesis®. Reflections on the Journey.* Also available in German.

- Lammers, Willem (2021). *Alone to Alive. Logosynthesis® and the Energy of Beliefs.* Also available in German.

35.2 Raya Williams MSc.

I graduated from Roehampton Institute (now University of Surrey) in 1998, with a degree in Psychology and Counseling. I later went on to study a master's in psychology, an Innovation and Design thinking Diploma (Emeritus), and more recently I became a Practitioner and Instructor in Logosynthesis.

I've worked in various business and therapeutic environments over the years but became frustrated that most models of healing and creativity don't acknowledge or include the spiritual dimension of our human experience. I discovered Logosynthesis while healing from a serious and debilitating illness; it was the breakthrough I'd been searching for, and I have practiced it ever since. I didn't look back.

This led to me launching my own private practice in January 2021 where I guide and support my clients as they heal from traumatic experiences, resolve limiting beliefs, and melt creative blocks away—all with the amazing healing power of words.

In recent years, I've contributed to various writing and editing projects including several other Logosynthesis books with Willem. Others have included the story of an innovative nursing model in the Netherlands and a personal journey of healing from cancer. One day I'm going to write my own book!

I also like to play in my little art studio, making mixed media artwork, writing, and generally experimenting. I enjoy walking in nature and any kind of cake.

Feel free to reach out with any questions, comments, or enquiries about working with me; I'd love to hear from you!

Visit my website at: www.logosynthesis.works

Follow me on Facebook at: www.facebook.com/LogosynW

36 THANK YOU!

Writing any book first begins with an idea driven by a mission. That idea gradually transforms into words, sentences, paragraphs, and chapters, over the course of days, months, or even years. Yet, for it to be able to make an impact, it must reach the world; and even the most prolific author cannot accomplish this feat alone.

Raya and I would like to express our sincere gratitude to everyone who contributed to this book. You have helped us to build on the foundations of earlier Logosynthesis books by incorporating insights from our experiences with Logosynthesis Master Practitioner candidates and the participants in the online Move On project. To Luzia, who cared for us, to our friends, family, colleagues, and mentors, your support and insights played a crucial role in shaping our work and helping us to uncover deeper truths. Thank you, Eric Robins for your careful editing and proofreading, thanks Ian Dennis for your patience and skill in visualizing our words in cover design and typesetting, thank you, Clarence Hamilton, for your continued support; and thank you to numerous others for feedback and proofreading. To those no longer on Earth, we thank you, and we miss you.

A special acknowledgment goes to those who explored the Void together with us, sharing their experiences and wisdom: Adrienne Moumin, Johan Reinhoudt, Cathy Schenkels-Caswell, Virna Trivellato, and Gerrie Wolffe. Your courage and openness allowed us to refine our model and methods, and this will benefit so many others seeking growth and transformation. We love your contributions, and this book is a tribute to our combined efforts and dedication.

37   A DISCLAIMER

We have used our best efforts in preparing and publishing this book. The book provides general information and is intended for educational purposes only. Logosynthesis is a novel approach to healing and development, but its full effectiveness, risks, and benefits remain unknown. By reading this book and using the presented techniques, the reader assumes full responsibility for any associated risks.

The content and techniques in this book may lead to emotional or physical sensations or bring up unresolved memories, which could be perceived as negative side effects. Emotional material might continue to surface after applying the described methods, indicating that other issues may need attention. Additionally, previously vivid or traumatic memories may fade, potentially affecting your ability to provide detailed legal testimony about a traumatic event.

The content of this book is not intended to diagnose, treat, cure, or prevent any disease or psychological disorder, and it should not replace medical or psychological treatment. The exercises, case reports, and information presented do not guarantee any specific outcome when using the Logosynthesis techniques for any issue. The information in this book is for your personal use only.

To apply Logosynthesis with others, you must be trained and qualified as a Logosynthesis Practitioner or Master Practitioner. While all materials and links to other resources are shared in good faith, the accuracy, validity, effectiveness, completeness, or usefulness of the provided information cannot be guaranteed. The authors accept no responsibility or liability for the use or misuse of the information in this book. If any court rules that any part of this disclaimer is invalid, the remaining parts will still apply.

We make no representations or warranties as to the accuracy, applicability, fitness, or completeness of the contents of this book. We disclaim all warranties (express or implied) of merchantability or fitness for a particular purpose. In no event shall we be liable for any loss or damage, including but not limited to special, incidental, consequential or other damages. Before implementing any protocol or opinion expressed in this book or making any health decisions, seek the advice of a competent medical, psychotherapeutic, legal, or other professional.

By continuing to read this book, you agree to all the above.

WE HELP YOU

Since the process described in this book can be challenging, we have created a dedicated Facebook group with the purpose of supporting you on the path to shaping your own reality. That group will offer opportunities to share your experiences with the material presented in this book, read about the experience of others, provide answers to your questions, and show you next possible steps.

You can join this Move On group through the following link:

https://www.facebook.com/groups/297950826456719

Please consider that individual coaching, counseling, or psychotherapy through this group cannot be provided. You find a list of experienced professionals on the webpage of the Logosynthesis International Association: www.logosynthesis.international/en/professionals/

If you're interested in learning more about Logosynthesis and its applications, you find more information on the website of the Logosynthesis International Association:

www.logosynthesis.international/en/seminare/

You can also join one of our Logosynthesis support groups on Facebook:

In English: www.facebook.com/groups/146545812063124

In French: www.facebook.com/groups/213984071955702

In German: www.facebook.com/groups/124570130943959

In Italian: www.facebook.com/groups/179934969371879

In Dutch: www.facebook.com/groups/830415237549711

If you would rather share your experiences with us in an email, feel free. You can reach us through www.willem.lammers.ch/write.

Have you found value in reading "Shaping Reality," and would you consider helping others discover it too? Many people choose their next book based on recommendations from trusted sources or reviews they come across. Your assistance in sharing your experience would be greatly appreciated.

Sharing your thoughts is simple; just talk to your friends about it. Mention one or two aspects of the book that you found valuable and explain why you think it's worth reading.

If you're feeling more ambitious, you can delve deeper into your experience. Share what challenges or problems you had before reading the book and how it helped you address them differently. You can even express any suggestions or changes you wish had been made to the book.

Posting a review is encouraged, and it's nearly as straight-forward as discussing it with a friend. Write a few sentences summarizing your thoughts and post them wherever you usu-ally read reviews—whether it's on Amazon, Goodreads, your personal blog, or any other platform where books are sold.

To make it easier for you, here's a link to my author page on Amazon:
https://www.amazon.com/stores/Willem-Lammers/author/B00J30IQRW

Just click on any book cover image, and it will lead you to the review page.

With deep gratitude and appreciation,

Willem and Raya

P.S. If you take a few extra minutes to let me know where and when you post your review, I will personally thank you for helping us reach new readers. Just drop me a message through willem.lammers.ch/write.

NOTES

[1] John 1:1.

[2] Gen 1:3.

[3] John 1:14.

[4] Sigmund Freud, Letter to W. Fliess, 25th May 1895.

[5] URL: https://reflections.yale.edu/article/seize-day-vocation-calling-work/i-live-my-life-widening-circles. Last accessed at 05.07.2022.

[6] https://genius.com/Bob-dylan-every-grain-of-sand-lyrics. Last accessed at 09.02.2023.

[7] https://www.goodreads.com/quotes/32265. Last accessed at 12.09.2021.

[8] URL: https://www.youtube.com/watch?v=zE7PKRjrid4. Last accessed 25.08.2023.

[9] Antonio Machado. https://www.goodreads.com/quotes/289625. Last accessed 25.08.2023.

[10] https://www.goodreads.com/quotes/125537. Last accessed 06.11.2023.

[11] Pilgrimage: https://en.wikipedia.org/wiki/Pilgrimage. Last accessed at 13.06.2023.

[12] David Hawkins (2014). *Power vs. Force. The Hidden Determinants of Human Behavior*. Hay House.

[13] URL: https://sites.pitt.edu/~dash/grimm019.html. Last accessed at 29.06.2023.

[14] URL: https://www.goodreads.com/quotes/126072-if-you-bring-forth-what-is-within-you-what-you. Last accessed at 20.04.2023.

[15] Lammers, Willem, with Raya Williams (2021). *Alone to Alive. Logosynthesis and the Energy of Beliefs*. Bad Ragaz, Switzerland: The Origin of Logosynthesis®.

[16] Charles Bukowski in: *A Little Book of Essential Quotes on Life, Art, and Love*. URL: https://books.google.ch/books/about/Charles_Bukowski.htm. Last accessed 31.10.2023.

[17] McGilchrist, Iain (2023) *The Matter with Things Vol.1*. Perspectiva Press.

[18] URL: https://en.wikipedia.org/wiki/Vesica_piscis. Last accessed at 20.04.2023.

[19] Lammers, Willem, with Raya Williams (2021). *Alone to Alive. Logosynthesis and the Energy of Beliefs*. Bad Ragaz, Switzerland: The Origin of Logosynthesis®.

[20] If you're unfamiliar with this procedure, read the description in Chapter 34 in the appendix.

[21] Ediho Lokanga (2020). A SPECIAL RELATIONSHIP BETWEEN MATTER, ENERGY, INFORMATION, AND CONSCIOUSNESS. URL: https://wireilla.com/physics/ijrap/papers/9320ijrap01.pdf. Last accessed at 12.07.2022.

[22] URL: https://www.goodreads.com/author/quotes/22039983.Rajesh_Goyal. Last accessed 29.08.2023.

[23] URL: https://www.brainyquote.com/quotes/maya_angelou_120859. Last accessed 29.08.2023.

[24] Joan Borysenko in a video published by the Shift Network.

[25] Joseph Campbell. URL: https://www.goodreads.com/quotes/44610-a-bit-of-advice-given-to-a-young-native-american. Last accessed 11.07.2022.

[26] URL: https://www.merriam-webster.com/dictionary/courage. Last accessed 05.02.2022.

[27] URL: https://www.dictionary.com/browse/courage. Last accessed 05.02.2022.

[28] Bandler, Richard, and Grinder, John (2005). *The Structure of Magic*. Science and Behavior Books.

[29] For a list of Logosynthesis books by Willem Lammers, see URL: www.logo-synthesis.net/reading. Last accessed 01.01.2023.

[30] URL: https://jkrishnamurti.org/about-dissolution-speech. Accessed at 09.11.2022.

[31] URL: https://www.brainyquote.com/quotes/h_p_lovecraft_676245. Last accessed 05.02.2022.

[32] Source unknown.

[33] URL: https://en.wikipedia.org/wiki/Horror_vacui_(art). Last accessed 01.01.2023.

[34] Lammers, Willem. The Seven Deadly Sins. A Logosynthesis Master Class. Bergamo, 2012.

[35] URL: https://en.wikipedia.org/wiki/Sloth_(deadly_sin)#cite_note-9. Last accessed at 14.07.2022.

[36] URL: www.logosynthesis.net/reading. Last accessed at 26.04.2023.

[37] Willem Lammers, seminar handouts.

[38] Lesser, Elizabeth. Midwives of the Soul Facebook Group. https://www.facebook.com/midwivesofthesoul Last accessed: 30.10.23.

[39] URL: https://www.deutschelyrik.de/schlaeft-ein-lied-in-allen-dingen.383.html. Accessed 08/25/2023. Translation by Willem Lammers.

[40] URL: www.goodreads.com/quotes/9085645. Last accessed 30.08.2023.

[41] Poem by John O'Donoghue, quoted in URL: https://www.themarginalian.org/2023/12/30/john-odonohue-blessings-beginnings/. Last accessed 02.01.2024.

[42] URL: https://donnaashworth.com/2021/02/01/dont-prioritise-your-looks/. Last accessed 07/12/2023.

[43] URL: https://www.thoughtco.com/semantic-satiation-1691937. Last accessed 22.05.2023.

[44] Willem Lammers (2021). *Alone to Alive.*

[45] The Basic Procedure in the Appendix is described in Willem Lammers' *Discover Logosynthesis®, Self-Coaching with Logosynthesis,* and in *Logosynthesis – a Handbook.* URL: www.logosynthesis.net/reading. Last accessed 16.05.2023.

[46] You find descriptions of the Bricks and Lego techniques in *Alone to Alive.* URL: www.logosynthesis.net/reading. Last accessed 16.05.2023.

[47] As described in: *Discover Logosynthesis®* by Willem Lammers. URL: www.logosynthesis.net/reading.

[48] You can also use the following URL for a short description of the protocol: https://www.logosynthesis.net/move-on-quick-reference/

[49] Shrek quote: URL: https://www.facebook.com/watch/?v=650206031847345. Last accessed 02.01.2024.

[50] This quote is probably derived from Joseph Campbell. URL: https://notesread.com/joseph-campbell-becoming-transparent-to-the-transcendent. Accessed at 06.07.2022.

[51] Desiderata. (2022, October 11). In URL: Wikipedia. https://en.wikipedia.org/wiki/Desiderata. Last acccessed 10.11.2022.

[52] URL: https://jkrishnamurti.org/about-dissolution-speech. Accessed 10.11.2022.

[53] There are many variations of this story, e.g. URL: http://joyfuldays.com/trust-in-god-but-tie-up-your-camel/. Accessed 10.11.2022.

[54] This version URL: https://www.anniewright.com/trust-god-tie-camel/. Accessed 10.11.2022.

[55] URL: https://libquotes.com/franz-kafka/quote/lbj7d0u. Accessed at 31.10.2022.

[56] URL: https://libquotes.com/gertrude-stein. Accessed 31.10.2022.

[57] URL: https://www.goodreads.com/quotes/997789. Accessed 10.11.2022.

[58] Jean-Jacques Rousseau in *The Social Contract*. URL: https://en.wikipedia.org/wiki/The_Social_Contract. Last accessed 07/26/2023.

[59] URL: https://www.goodreads.com/quotes/45978. Accessed 07/25/2023.

[60] URL: https://www.goodreads.com/quotes/201777. Accessed 03.11.2022.

[61] URL: https://www.azquotes.com/quote/848040. Last accessed at 25.05.2023.

[62] Adapted from URL: https://www.goodreads.com/quotes/292417-every-morning-in-africa-a-gazelle-wakes-up-it-knows. Last accessed 05/05/2023.

[63] URL: https://beyondthenotes.org/artmusic/okeeffe/tocreate.html. Accessed at 03.02.2022.

[64] From *Kafka on the Shore*. URL: https://www.goodreads.com/quotes/315361. Accessed 20.07.2023.

[65] Often misattributed to Eleanor Roosevelt. URL: https://www.goodreads.com/quotes/3929. Last accessed 25.05.2023.

[66] URL: https://www.youtube.com/watch?v=qYkEvusvQv4. Accessed 02.11.2022.

[67] URL: https://www.goodreads.com/quotes/195356. Last accessed at 02.11.2023

[68] In the Tao Te Ching. URL: https://www.bbc.co.uk/religion/religions/taoism/beliefs/tao.shtml. Last accessed at 06.07.2022.

[69] Rainer Maria Rilke: Über die Geduld. URL: https://www.themarginalian.org/2012/06/01/rilke-on-questions/. Last accessed at 26.07.2023.

[70] URL: https://sacredmoves.com/general/the-blessings-of-john-odonohue/. Last accessed 25.07.2023.

[71] The following URL contains a short description of the protocol to download and print: https://www.logosynthesis.net/move-on-quick-reference/

[72] Berne, E. (1982). *A Layman's Guide to Psychiatry and Psychoanalysis.* Simon & Schuster.

[73] You find an overview of Willem Lammers' books under the URL: www.logosynthesis.net/reading.

[74] Lammers, Willem (2015). *Self-Coaching with Logosynthesis®.* CreateSpace.

[75] If you want to learn more about the Logosynthesis Basic Procedure, we recommend Willem Lammers' book *Discover Logosynthesis®* as a first step.

[76] You find a list of certified professionals on the website of the Logosynthesis International Association: www.logosynthesis.international/professionals.

[77] URL: https://www.youtube.com/channel/UCuv5yoDbntXGCzC5pd2gy1Q/playlists. Last accessed at 03.10.2021.

Made in United States
Troutdale, OR
08/19/2024

22141079R00166